THE OAKWOOD LIBRARY OF RAILWAY HISTORY   OL160

The Axminster & Lyme Regis Light Railway

Peter Paye

THE OAKWOOD PRESS

© Oakwood Press & Peter Paye 2015

British Library Cataloguing in Publication Data
A Record for this book is available from the British Library
ISBN 978 0 85361 739 6

Typeset by Oakwood Graphics.
Repro by PKmediaworks, Cranborne, Dorset.
Printed by Gomer Press, Llandysul, Ceredigion.

All rights reserved. No part of this book may be reproduced or transmitted in any form or by any means, electronic or mechanical, including photocopying, recording or by any information storage and retrieval system, without permission from the Publisher in writing.

Lyme Regis publicity notice.

Front cover: '415' class 4-4-2T No. 30582 arrives at Lyme Regis with the branch train from Axminster on a sunny day in August 1960. *Author*
Title page: A period view of the harbour entrance and the Cobb at Lyme Regis.
Author's Collection
Rear cover: One inch Ordnance Survey map, 1946 edition, showing the route of the railway from Axminster to Lyme Regis. *Crown Copyright*

Published by The Oakwood Press (Usk), P.O. Box 13, Usk, Mon., NP15 1YS.
E-mail: sales@oakwoodpress.co.uk
Website: www.oakwoodpress.co.uk

Contents

	Introduction	5
Chapter One	Construction and Opening	7
Chapter Two	London & South Western Ownership	29
Chapter Three	Southern Railway Operation	35
Chapter Four	Nationalization and Closure	43
Chapter Five	The Route Described	59
Chapter Six	Permanent Way, Signalling and Staff	85
Chapter Seven	Timetables and Traffic	97
Chapter Eight	Locomotives and Rolling Stock	113
Appendix One	Bridges	140
Appendix Two	Level Crossings	142
	Acknowledgements	143
	Bibliography	143
	Index	144

A nostagic scene at Lyme Regis as passengers gather on the platform awaiting the arrival of the incoming service. Two loaded barrows of luggage stand waiting the attention of the station staff once the train pulls in to the platform. *Oakwood Collection*

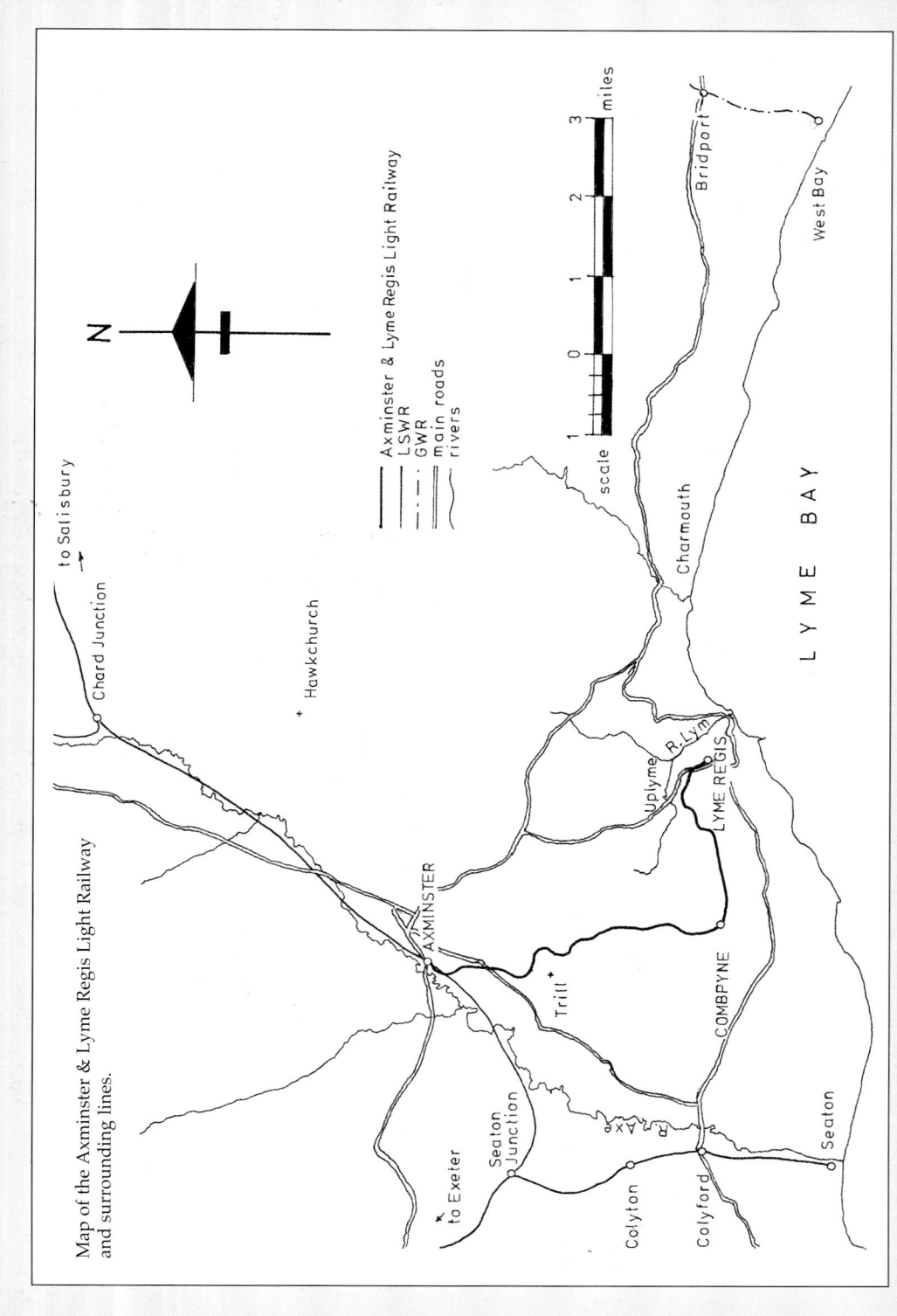

Map of the Axminster & Lyme Regis Light Railway and surrounding lines.

Introduction

For centuries Lyme Regis was noted for its beautiful setting, and continues as 'a gem of the Dorset coast'. Jane Austen found the town enchanting and in *Persuasion* wrote 'a very strange stranger it must be who does not see charms in the immediate environs of Lyme ... the happiest spot ... for sitting in unwearied contemplation.' Millions since have enjoyed the charms of Lyme Regis and the Jurassic Coast and, although not the easiest of places to access by road in the 19th and early 20th century, for 62 years many took the opportunity to travel to the coast by rail on the branch line from Axminster. Whilst the majority were attracted by the natural beauty of the area, its coastline, sea and sand, on the border of the counties of Devon and Dorset, for the railway enthusiast the appeal was to travel behind veteran locomotives, which had been used on the branch for five decades.

The curvature and steep gradients encountered on the light railway presented difficulties with motive power and after early trials and tribulations the London & South Western Railway (LSWR) and later Southern Railway (SR) and British Railways (BR) found the Adams '415' class 4-4-2 tank locomotives dating from 1882, suitably modified to satisfy the weight restrictions imposed by the respective civil engineers, suitable for the task. Their reign was interrupted on occasions when management attempted to find alternatives but the ever-ageing machines continued unmolested until the early 1960s. The sound of their 'throaty pant' as they tackled the gradients will live in the memory of many. Only at the last were they beyond redemption and replaced by London Midland Region (LMR) class '2MT' 2-6-2 tank engines but their stay was short for the infamous Beeching Report recommended closure of the line and they succumbed to encroaching diesel-multiple-units (dmus) before the final death.

The publication of this book coincides with the 50th anniversary of the closure of the erstwhile Axminster & Lyme Regis Light Railway linking Axminster on the LSWR main line in Devon to Lyme Regis in Dorset. Before the coming of the railway Lyme Regis was a fashionable holiday resort with an historic past. After the opening of the Salisbury to Exeter line in 1860 local factions pressed for a rail connection to the coast but failure to connect with the expanding railway network led to the threat of economic stagnation. Despite many attempts over a period of five decades, geographical difficulties and lack of financial funds deterred would-be developers and it was not until the passing of the Light Railways Act in 1896 that interested parties gathered enough support to build a line. By 1899 the Light Railway Order was duly obtained and, with the 'blessing and backing of the LSWR', progress was assured.

Construction was entrusted to Arthur C. Pain, an eminent light railway engineer who had supervised various schemes including the Culm Valley Light Railway between Tiverton Junction and Hemyock in Devon and the 3 ft gauge Southwold Railway in Suffolk. The works included the spanning of the Cannington valley by a viaduct, constructed chiefly of concrete and one of the earliest such structures in the country. The railway opened with great celebration in August 1903 but early receipts were disappointing as speed perforce was restricted to a maximum of 25 mph, and in 1907 the company was taken over by the LSWR, who then worked the line as one of their many branches. The railway, however, served its purpose by lifting the depression from the area for the regular flow of local traffic was supplemented by the arrival and departure of holidaymakers in high summer, when through coaches were worked to and from London Waterloo.

As a result of the 1921 Railways Act the erstwhile light railway became part of the Southern Railway from 1st January, 1923 and the new regime over the next decade, whilst carrying out improvements to Axminster and Lyme Regis stations, sought to rationalize the operating costs of running the branch. Summer Saturdays saw the continued working of through coaches from London Waterloo and holidays by the sea provided encouraging passenger receipts, but winter services were poorly patronized. Signalling at Combpyne was finally abolished, completing a programme commenced by the LSWR in 1921,when the crossing loop was converted to a siding. The employment of a guard on passenger services was dispensed with on any train of three coaches or less and early morning, late evening weekday trains, and some Sunday trains were replaced by Southern National buses, the SR having a shareholding in the company. The line entered nationalization from 1st January, 1948 but initially few changes were made save for minor improvements in coaching stock and wagons, and motive power remained unaltered. As the years progressed it became obvious improvements were necessary: modernization was the watchword on British Railways and the ancient Adams '415' class 4-4-2 tank locomotives were increasingly costly to maintain. Revenue was declining, except during the summer months. Built to serve an area with a population of less than 6,000, passenger traffic potential was minimal and heavily reliant on imports for freight, the branch ultimately failed to withstand the competition of road transport. Unfortunately the railway, because of geographical difficulties and lack of funds, was forced to terminate over half a mile distant and 250 ft above the town of Lyme Regis a factor, which weighed heavily against potential traffic in later years. Likewise the one intermediate station, Combpyne, was located in an isolated area far from any sizeable habitation thus attracting little traffic. Closure of the line was rumoured for several years as the branch was an expensive luxury the cost-conscious BR could ill afford; confirmation came with the infamous Beeching Report of 1963 that closure was under consideration. Hopes of salvation were dashed when the line was transferred from the Southern Region to the Western Region in January of that year. Replacement steam traction offered some hope but steps were well advanced, freight traffic being withdrawn on 3rd February, 1964, and after the obligatory Transport Users' Consultative Committee (TUCC) hearing, objections to closure were overruled and the Minister of Transport authorized BR to effect complete closure of the line on and from Monday 29th November, 1965. The last trains ran on 28th November, leaving the supposedly more convenient and direct bus service as the only public transport between the two towns.

I have attempted to trace the fascinating history of the Axminster & Lyme Regis Light Railway from conception to closure and details have been checked with available documents, but apologies are offered for any errors, which might have occurred.

Peter Paye
Bishop's Stortford

Chapter One

Construction and Opening

Lyme Regis, a picturesque coastal town, situated at the south-western extremity of Dorset on its border with Devon, has a population of approximately 4,000. Overlooking Lyme Bay and at the mouth of the River Lim or Lym nestling in a combe between two rocky hills and surrounded by heights of 450 feet, the area first came to notice in 774 when Cenwulf of Wessex gave land near the river to the monks of Sherborne Abbey for salt boiling. By 1279 the town had gained such importance that it became a Royal Borough returning two Members of Parliament until the Reform Act of 1832. The famous Cobb, a stone-built combination of pier, quay and breakwater, was built in the reign of Edward I and by the reign of Edward III the town possessed a sizeable sea-going community trading with distant ports. After the sending of four ships to aid the siege of Calais, the French retaliated and sacked the town. Rebuilt Lyme, of strategic importance during the Civil War, was the landing place of the Duke of Monmouth during the rebellion on 11th June, 1685, in his ill-fated attempt to take the crown from his uncle, James II. The French Revolution again ruined cross-channel trading and local industries, including lace making and weaving, ceased as the town's prosperity declined. By 1750 Lyme had again recovered to become a fashionable resort second only to Bath, and a decade later the town acquired its first bathing machine and the assembly rooms were opened. However, with the advent of rail travel to the south-west, popularity again declined. Promoters were keen, however, to provide the area with such a facility, to improve trade and conditions, and in 1845 several abortive railway schemes were mooted.

The first of these, the Bristol & English Channels Direct Junction Railway, envisaged a line from Stoke Canon on the Bristol & Exeter Railway via Watchet, Ottery St Mary, Honiton and Axminster to Bridport, passing close to Lyme. The Bristol & Exeter Railway backed a proposal by the Exeter Great Western Railway, by extending their Berks & Hants line from Hungerford to Westbury from where the new company hoped to secure powers to extend westward to Exeter, at the same time building a branch from Axminster to Bridport. The third scheme, proposed by the Bristol and English Channels Connection Railway, suggested a route from a new harbour at Stofford near Burnham-on-Sea via Bridgwater, Taunton and Ilminster from where one branch was to run to Bridport harbour and the other to Lyme Regis via Chard and Axminster. Finally the Lyme Regis & Taunton Railway proposed a direct route between Lyme Bay on the English Channel coast and an undisclosed point on the Bristol Channel coast. This company actually issued a Prospectus but never got as far as being surveyed and, as with the other schemes, fell into oblivion.

Two years elapsed before schemes were again revived, when the London & South Western Railway supported the Exeter, Yeovil & Dorchester Railway in their plans to connect the places named, in direct opposition to the Salisbury & Yeovil Railway, which was also backed by the LSWR. This rather puzzling decision to support rival factions was part of the LSWR policy to stop a revised Exeter Great Western Railway plan to force a branch line to Charmouth. The hilly nature of the southern coastal route prohibited the scheme because of costs and the northern route, being extensively cheaper, was constructed from Salisbury to Yeovil and Exeter Queen Street, completed and opened on 19th July, 1860.

One of the stations between Salisbury and Exeter was Chard Road, later Chard Junction, which served the Somerset town of Chard some two miles to the north. In 1863 the Chard Road & Lyme Regis Railway proposed a line between the two points via the Blackwater valley towards Birdsmoorgate continuing via a branch line to the Cobb at Lyme. Another extension involved a branch from Birdsmoorgate to Bridport but residents of the latter town objected. Despite the hilly nature of the terrain to be crossed, application was actually made to Parliament in 1864 but was withdrawn after opposition from the Great Western Railway (GWR) and LSWR. The plan was resurrected in the same year with the title reversed as the Lyme Regis & Chard Road Railway, following a more direct route, but again Parliament threw out the proposition, for failing to comply with standing orders. Also in 1864 the Lyme Regis Junction Railway was proposed leaving the LSWR main line south of Chard Road and running direct to Lyme Regis. This proposal was significant in that an impressive terminus was planned adjacent to the town cemetery and also the company planned a tramway from the station to run along the Cobb, a man-made breakwater protecting the small harbour. This again was rejected by Parliament as was the Bridport, Lyme & Axminster Railway, which was basically a revision of the 1845 scheme for a coastal route from Bridport to Axminster with a branch from the hamlet of Monkton Wyld to Lyme Regis.

In 1865 yet more attempts were made to bring the railway to Lyme Regis. The Lyme Regis & Axminster Joint or Junction Railway was a scheme for a branch to depart from the LSWR main line a short distance north of Axminster and their proposal included a branch to the Cobb but not along the structure. Another scheme, the Bridport, Lyme & South Coast Railway, essentially an extension of the Bridport Railway, which had opened to traffic in 1857, proposed to exploit the coastal region of west Dorset and east Devon connecting Bridport to a junction with the LSWR south of Chard Road and incorporating a branch to Lyme Regis from a junction near Whitechurch Canonicorum. Again both failed, the former attracting little support whilst the latter, although making provision for the GWR and LSWR to subscribe, actually reached the Lords before withdrawal.

In the meantime a significant step was taken in 1870 to bring a transport connection to the coast when John Groves of the Royal Lion Hotel, Lyme Regis entered into an agreement with the LSWR to provide a horse-bus service to Axminster station. This would run twice daily to meet the 12.57 pm and 3.08 pm arrivals from London, considered the busiest trains of the day from Waterloo. The service quickly became known as the Lyme Regis Railway Bus.

Almost five years elapsed before a further railway scheme was raised by the Lyme Regis Railway Company to connect the town with the LSWR main line at Axminster. After the GWR had withdrawn its opposition on 22nd March, 1871 the promoters concluded an agreement with the LSWR to work the line for half the gross receipts. The Bill had an uneventful passage through Parliament and received the Royal Assent on 14th August, 1871 (34 and 35 Vict. cap. 190), granting powers to construct a line from Axminster to Lyme Regis via Uplyme, 7 miles 30 chains in length. Estimated to cost £86,000 the actual authorized route was via Combpyne, considered to be the cheapest but by no means shortest option, following for most of the way the contours of the land and eliminating the construction of tunnels.

The Prospectus enthused,

> This company has been established for the purpose of making a railway from a point commencing with the Axminster station of the LSWR and terminating at a point near

the parish church of Lyme Regis, which will thus be placed in unbroken communication with the Metropolis and all the principal towns in the United Kingdom. The want of railway communication with the justly celebrated watering place of Lyme Regis has long been felt.

No problems were envisaged attracting traffic although regret was expressed concerning the loss of coal, hemp and timber to other ports. It was doubted that the traffic would return once the new rail link was established and it was thought good quality north country coal would be brought to Lyme Regis by sea for onward conveyance to inland towns, which up to now had made do with inferior South Wales coal. It continued:

> A very large traffic in fish and vegetable produce would spring into existence concurrently with the establishment of railway communication between London and the interior. Important cement works have been erected near Lyme Regis and proper facilities for the despatch of the materials, which the district yields in abundance will give an immense impetus to this manufacture.

Three years elapsed, however, before the ceremony of the cutting of the first sod was performed on Tuesday 29th September, 1874. Despite heavy rain in the morning the day was almost a public holiday in Lyme Regis with flags and bunting decorating the various premises in Broad Street, and the bells of St Michael's church ringing at intervals. From the Royal Lion Hotel, decorated with evergreens and flowers, the local band led a procession which included the Mayor Dr Skinner, Mayoress, Mrs Skinner, Members of the Corporation, Ralph Ward Jackson, Chairman of the Company, H. Kember, the Company Secretary and W.E. Duncan, a solicitor, representatives of the engineers, Nimmo & Macnay and others including navvy Benjamin Mills dressed in his finery, to the site of the ceremony, a field called Higher Early Mead owned by Mr Healey. By the time the procession arrived the rain had stopped and at 2.00 pm Mrs Skinner, the Mayoress, wife of Dr Skinner, performed the actual deed using a ceremonial spade on the blade of which was inscribed 'Lyme Regis Railway'. The earth was placed into an ornate miniature wheelbarrow, which was later presented to Mrs Skinner. After the ceremony the procession returned to the Royal Lion Hotel where 120 invited guests attended a ceremonial luncheon.

Confidence in the railway grew and in the following Parliamentary session application was made to extend the facilities at Lyme Regis and continue the line via Marshwood Vale to Bridport, with a short branch to Bridport Harbour at West Bay. The Bill passed through the Commons but was withdrawn in the Lords, and as a result of further inactivity due to difficulty in raising capital the original powers were allowed to lapse in 1876, leaving Lyme in continued railway isolation.

Petitions to the LSWR in 1882 and 1887 for backing to build a line met with outright refusal, leaving the inhabitants of Lyme Regis increasingly incensed by the failure of these and other futile schemes, which had been mooted over the intervening years. The difficulty of penetrating the terrain between the LSWR main line and Lyme Regis involving extensive and costly earthworks precluded any further ambitious plans. Then in 1896 Parliament gave agreement to a statute that was to help overcome the problem. The Light Railways Act of 1896 was promoted to alleviate the distress of the agricultural depression by allowing inexpensive railways to be constructed in rural areas, with the proviso that those so constructed would be

AXMINSTER AND LYME REGIS LIGHT RAILWAY.

ESTIMATE OF EXPENSE

Line No. 1.	Miles.	f.	ch.		Whether Single or Double.
Length of Line	6	4			Single.

	Cubic yds.	Price per yd.	£	s.	d.	£	s.	d.
Earthworks:								
Cuttings—Rock	...							
Soft Soil	225,311	1s.	11,265	11	0			
Roads	2,798	1s. 6d.	209	17	0			
Total	228,109		11,475	8	0	11,475	8	0

Embankments, including Roads—218,770 *Cubic yards*.

		£	s.	d.
Bridges—Public Roads . . . . . *Number* 7 .		3,550	0	0
Accommodation Bridges and Works		1,632	0	0
Viaducts		5,650	0	0
Culverts and Drains and *retaining* Walls *of Roads* . . .		1,150	0	0
Metalling and Level Crossings		120	8	0
Gatekeepers' Houses at Level Crossings . . .				
Permanent Way including Fencing				

Miles	f.	c.	Cost per Mile. £ s. d.				
6	4	5-60	1,887 0 0	12,397	13	0

	£	s.	d.
Permanent Way for Sidings and Cost of Junctions . .	1,200	0	0
Stations	550	0	0
	37,725	9	0
Contingencies . . . . . . 10 per cent.	3,772	11	0
	41,498	0	0

	A.	R.	P.			
Land and Buildings	47	1	25	. . .	7,909	0	0

TOTAL . £	49,407	0	0

Witness—ROBERT NUNN.   ARTHUR C. PAIN, *Engineer*.

freed from the obligation to build to the high standards laid down by the Board of Trade (BoT) for main lines. Section 5 of the Act stated that where the Board of Agriculture certified the provision of a light railway would benefit agriculture the Treasury might agree to aid the building of the line out of public money. The clause included the essential paragraph that where 'a necessary means of communication would be established between a fishing harbour and a market, or that such railway is necessary for the development or maintenance of some definite industry' then finance would be made available. Unfortunately, despite investigating this option the Lyme Regis scheme could not be construed as wholly benefiting from this clause. However, another significant feature was that 'application to the Light Railway Commissioners for an order could be made by the county, borough or district through which the railway would pass, or by any company or individual'. Thus the way was open and the Mayor of Lyme, H.O. Bickley, chaired a meeting at the Town Hall in August 1897 when an invited guest, W.S. Sebright Green, head of a London firm of solicitors, spoke of the need for a railway in the area to save Lyme Regis from economic stagnation. Very little progress was made until the people of Axminster added their support at a meeting convened by W.E. Pitfield Chapple, a solicitor and Chairman of the parish council, chaired by William Forward, and held in the parish church school on 25th March. 1898. As a result a petition, reputedly 20 yards long and containing 1,630 names was sent to the LSWR Directors advocating the construction of a railway linking Axminster and Lyme Regis. But despite promises to consider the application, the scheme came to naught.

In the meantime Chard Town Council at a meeting chaired by the Mayor, Alderman A. Venables Kyrke, on Thursday 26th May, 1898, resurrected a proposal for a light railway from Chard Junction to Lyme Regis via Hawkchurch, with the possibility of a tramway extension from the terminus to Charmouth, but as with other schemes this attempt came to nothing. The LSWR had also taken steps to improve facilities at the junction and Colonel F.A. Marindin inspected the new up refuge siding at Axminster on 10th November, 1898. He found it was served by trailing points from the up main line. The siding was controlled from the signal box containing 16 working levers of which three were of the push and pull type. He duly recommended the use of the new siding as interlocking was satisfactory.

Undaunted the promoters of the Axminster to Lyme Regis line soon rallied and obtained amongst others the support of Sir Cuthbert Edgar Peek Bart, who lived in the cliff top estate at Rousdon near Combpyne, and was a prominent landowner in the area. Later the company's solicitors, Sebright Green and Williams of London, applied to the Light Railway Commissioners for an order for the Axminster & Lyme Regis Light Railway (A&LR) in November 1898, the embryonic company now having gained the support of the LSWR.

Opposition to the A&LR Light Railway order came from a committee backing the Bridport to Lyme Regis scheme, which had not itself reached the Parliamentary stage, and a Mr Allen, a resident of Lyme Regis, who objected to the siting of the terminal station, which he considered would 'injure the scenery' and depreciate the value of residential property. The Light Railway Commissioners dismissed the former and pointed out to the latter that while the station was not ideally situated, its planned position had been dictated by local topography.

The Axminster and Lyme Regis Light Railway Order was authorized on 15th June, 1899 and gave the company powers to construct a line, Railway No. 1 – 6 miles 4 furlongs 5.60 chains or thereabouts in length, commencing in the parish of Axminster in the County of Devon near the footbridge on the up platform at

APPLICATION FORM FOR ORDINARY SHARES.

AXMINSTER & LYME REGIS LIGHT RAILWAY COMPANY,

Incorporated under the Axminster & Lyme Regis Light Railway Order 1899.

ISSUE OF

5,500 Shares of £10 each at par, bearing Interest during construction at the rate of £3 per cent. per annum.

To the Directors of

AXMINSTER AND LYME REGIS LIGHT RAILWAY COMPANY.

GENTLEMEN,

Having paid to the Company's Bankers the sum of £................., being the deposit of £2 per Share due on application for............... Shares of £10 each, I hereby request you to allot me the same, and I hereby agree to accept the same, or any less number allotted to me, and I agree to pay the instalments thereon, as required in the terms of the Prospectus, and I authorise you to place my name on the Register in respect of such Shares.

Name (in full)......................
(Mr., Mrs., or Miss.)

Address (in full)......................

Occupation......................

Date......................1900

(left margin:) WILLIAMS, DEACON, AND MANCHESTER & SALFORD BANK, LIMITED, Birchin Lane, London, E.C.; COMPANY, LIMITED, or to any of the Branches of these Banks.

AXMINSTER & LYME REGIS LIGHT RAILWAY COMPANY,

Incorporated under the Axminster & Lyme Regis Light Railway Order 1899.

ISSUE OF

5,500 SHARES OF £10 EACH AT PAR.

RECEIPT FOR DEPOSIT ON SHARES.

(TO BE RETURNED TO THE APPLICANT.)

Received the............day of............1900,

of............

the sum of............being the Deposit

of £2 per Share due on Application for............Shares.

For { WILLIAMS, DEACON, AND MANCHESTER & SALFORD BANK, LIMITED.
{ WILTS & DORSET BANKING COMPANY, LIMITED.

£   :   :

STAMP.

(left margin:) This Form must be sent entire with remittance to the Company's Bankers, or to the WILTS & DORSET BANKING

Axminster & Lyme Regis Light Railway application for shares.

Axminster LSWR station and terminating in the borough and parish of Lyme Regis in the County of Dorset in the southern angle of a field belonging to W.C. Cleave, in the occupancy of William Stapleforth and numbered 149 approximately half a mile from the town centre. A second line, Railway No. 2 – 1 furlong 1.60 chains or thereabouts in length wholly in the parish of Axminster in the County of Devon, was authorized commencing by a junction with the LSWR goods siding at Axminster station 15½ chains from the goods shed measured in a south-westerly direction and terminating by a junction with Railway No. 1 near the centre of a field belonging to the Trustees of Henry Knight, deceased, in the occupancy of Reuben Swain and numbered 956 in the said parish. Both railways were to be built to standard gauge of 4 ft 8½ in. The company was authorized to raise £55,000 in £10 shares together with a loan of £6,000, once £27,500 had been subscribed and another £6,000 when the full share issue was sold. Under clause 30(1) of the order the junction between the light railway and the LSWR at Axminster was to be made with the agreement and satisfaction of the main line company engineer whilst clause 30(4) stipulated 'the company shall carry railway No. 1 over the LSWR main line by means of a bridge of a span of not less than 26 feet 3 inches'. The provision of the order by clause 33 also allowed the company, with the agreement of the LSWR (but not otherwise) to run their

> … engines, carriages, waggons [sic] and trucks and their officers or servants whether in charge of engines or trains or for any other purpose whatsoever for the interchange of any traffic so much and such portion of the railway or sidings of the LSW Company as is situated between the junction of the Railway (No. 2) with the LSWR and Axminster station together with that station and all roads, platforms, points, signals, water, water engines, engine sheds, standing room for engines, booking and other offices, warehouses, sidings, junctions, machinery, works and conveniences of or connected with the said portion of the LSWR and station.

The maximum weight on any pair of wheels was limited to 12 tons if 56 lb. per yard rails were used, increased to 14 tons if 60 lb. per yard rails were employed on the line. Two years were permitted for the purchase of land and three years for the completion of works. The estimated total cost of constructing the railway was £49,938 8s. 0d. broken down as follows:

	£	s.	d.
Earthworks	11,615	17	0
Bridges and Viaducts	10,832	0	0
Culverts, retaining walls etc.	1,270	8	0
Permanent way	13,876	13	0
Stations	550	0	0
Land and buildings	7,979	0	0
Contingencies	3,814	10	0

Sir Cuthbert Edgar Peek Bart was appointed first Chairman of the company with fellow Directors John Reginald Charles Talbot of Rhode Hill, Uplyme and the Right Honourable Sir John Kennaway MP of Escott.

The contract for the building of the railway was awarded to Baldrey & Yerburgh of Westminster, London, SW1 who tendered at £36,542 0s. 0d. whilst Arthur C. Pain M.Inst.CE of 17 Victoria Street London SW1 was appointed Engineer and H.G. Swayne Williams of 17 Victoria Street Westminster, Secretary. W.S. Sebright Green

The List of Applications for Shares will be Closed on the Evening of Tuesday, the 24th April, 1900.

To be worked by the LONDON AND SOUTH WESTERN RAILWAY COMPANY, who guarantee a 10 per cent. Rebate on all through traffic passing over their Railway towards making up the dividend on these Shares to 4 per cent. in each year.

Axminster and Lyme Regis Light Railway Company.

Incorporated by the Axminster and Lyme Regis Light Railway Order, 1899.

By which the liability of the Shareholders is limited to the amount of their Shares.

Authorised Share Capital £55,000,

In 5,500 Shares of £10 each, the whole of which are now offered for subscription at par, payable as follows:—

On Application	- -	£2 0 0
On Allotment	- -	£2 0 0

The balance in calls of £2 each with an interval of not less than three months between each call.

Interest during construction will be paid at the rate of 3 per cent. per annum subject to the provisions of Section 56 of the Axminster and Lyme Regis Light Railway Order, 1899. Subscribers may pay up in full on Allotment or when any subsequent call is due, and interest will accrue on the amount prepaid.

Total Borrowing Powers £12,000 in 4 per cent. Debenture Stock.

Directors.

Col. R. WILLIAMS, M.P., *Chairman.*
H. H. J. W. DRUMMOND, Esq.,
F. J. MACAULAY, Esq.,
} DIRECTORS OF THE LONDON AND SOUTH WESTERN RAILWAY COMPANY.

SIR CUTHBERT EDGAR PEEK, BART., Rousdon, Devon.
JOHN REGINALD CHARLES TALBOT, Esq., Rhode Hill, Uplyme, Devon.

Bankers.

WILLIAMS, DEACON AND MANCHESTER AND SALFORD BANK, LIMITED, 20, Birchin Lane, London, E.C., and all Branches, and
WILTS AND DORSET BANKING COMPANY, LIMITED, Lyme Regis, and all Branches.

Engineer.

ARTHUR C. PAIN, Esq., M.Inst. C.E., 17, Victoria Street, S.W.

Solicitors.

Messrs. SEBRIGHT GREEN & CO., 5, Spring Gardens, Charing Cross, S.W.

Brokers.

Messrs. MORTIMER, SCOTTER & CO., 75, Lombard Street, and Stock Exchange, London, E.C.

Auditors.

Messrs. W. B. PEAT & CO., 3, Lothbury, London, E.C.

Secretary.

H. G. SWAYNE WILLIAMS, Esq.

Office.

17, VICTORIA STREET, S.W.

Axminster & Lyme Regis Light Railway notice of share issue.

& Company of 5 Spring Gardens, Charing Cross, London SW, solicitor, F. Scotter of Mortimer, Scotter & Company of 75 Lombard Street, London C, broker and Messrs W.B. Peat of 3 Lothbury London EC, auditors. The company's registered office was 17 Victoria Street, London SW, occupied by Pain. Pain had been involved with many schemes including the light railway from Tiverton Junction to Hemyock in Devon and the 3 ft gauge Southwold Railway in Suffolk opened in 1879. A.C. Pain employed his sons, Edward and Claude, both civil engineers, on the Lyme Regis scheme.

Monetary problems were solved when the LSWR, realizing the usefulness of the line, subscribed £25,000 towards construction costs and later on 4th April, 1900 agreed to work and manage the future railway in perpetuity, deducting 55 per cent and government duty from receipts, together with 4 per cent of the cost of the works, if provided, with the Axminster & Lyme Regis Light Railway taking the balance. The LSWR, however, consented to pay a 10 per cent rebate on through traffic if there were sufficient funds to pay 4 per cent on £55,000. Colonel R. Williams MP of Brideshead, H.H.J.W. Drummond of East Budleigh and F.J. Macauley of Alverstoke, Clapham Common, Directors of the LSWR, joined the Axminster & Lyme Regis Board to look after LSWR interests.

Construction of the line began on 19th June, 1900 and some of the heavier materials were brought by sea and off-loaded on the Cobb at Lyme Regis, the first consignment arriving in August on the ketch *Ida*. A local carrier, H.G. Lambert of Town Mills, was contracted to haul the materials from the Cobb to the works site. At the Board meeting held on 19th July, Arthur Pain reported that he had possession of 2½ miles of property to enable the contractor to commence work. Trial bore holes had been made at the summit of the line just beyond Combpyne which discovered sandy clay for the first 7 ft of depth followed by 23 ft of tough red marl with large quantities of flint closely packed together. Further towards Lyme Regis on the site of the proposed 10-arch Cannington viaduct, the Engineer and contractor had discovered nothing but sandy clay.

Whilst satisfactory progress was being made on the section of line between Axminster and Combpyne difficulties were mounting at Cannington. On 4th October, 1900 Pain reported the contractor had found the presence of peat and soft materials in places under piers 2, 3, 4, 6 and 7 and because of this discovery the foundations would require excavating to a greater width and depth, incurring an estimated additional cost of £235 over budget. However, a stone crusher had been erected and tested satisfactorily and concreting had commenced. Seventy-eight men were employed on construction but great difficulty was experience in finding labour. The viaduct, built of concrete, was comparable with Glenfinnan viaduct on the West Highland Railway constructed by 'Concrete Bob' Robert McAlpine and completed in 1901.

The combination of bad weather and undulating countryside delayed the works and greensand encountered in the cuttings, especially on the floor of the Cannington valley, caused slow progress. At the Board meeting on 2nd January, 1902 Pain advised the Directors of further delays especially on the construction of Cannington viaduct and elsewhere, notably at Walley or Whalley Lane bridge near Uplyme, where the contractor proposed the substitution of a timber bridge as it was lighter than the concrete structure *in situ*. The Directors expressed their disapproval of the continued delays and thought the contractors' representative had displayed a great want of forethought at the works 'in not having the materials ready for completing the viaduct as and when they were required'. The situation further deteriorated for on 5th March,

1902 Pain reported that work at the viaduct had been stopped for 14 days because of frost, adding to the eight days lost the previous month because of 'wet days'. The foundations of the bridge under the main road on the approach to Lyme Regis were in running sand, which was causing the contractor 'much difficulty'. However, he added some refreshing good news by advising that the steelwork for the bridge over the LSWR main line at Axminster and the nearby Musbury Road had been obtained and erected. The continuing delays forced the Board to seek approval for an extension of time for completion of the line. An application was duly made in May 1902 for an extension of 12 months to 15th September, 1903 for completion of works, under section 20 of the Light Railway Order.

On 14th May, 1902 the Engineer reported the completion of arches 6 to 10 of the viaduct and it was expected the remaining arches would be turned by the end of July. At the general meeting of the company held on 13th August, 1902, chaired by Colonel R. Williams, it was reported that £54,233 17s. 2d. had been expended on works to the end of June, and subsequent application was made to the Board of Trade seeking authority to increase the ordinary stock by £10,000 and debenture stock by £3,000.

By early January 1903 the works had reached such an advanced stage that arrangements were made for a special train to run on the line on Thursday 22nd January. Starting from the down main platform at Axminster and using the spur from the goods yard, the train was hauled by the locomotive loaned by the LSWR to the contractor, Beyer, Peacock 0-6-0 saddle tank No. 131. Aboard the special were Colonel Robert Williams MP, Sir John Kennaway Bart MP and J.R.C. Talbot. The remedial works on Cannington viaduct then precluded the contractor from running any trains across the structure and prevented ballasting of Lyme Regis station and its approaches although some work was achieved by using horse-drawn waggons hauled up from Lyme Regis on the poorly made roads.

The saga of Cannington viaduct continued into the New Year, exacerbated by inclement weather in April and May 1903. Pain reported on 27th May that the foundations of the abutment and No. 1 pier were constructed on dry sand and flint stones and below near the level of the bottom of the valley the sand was wet and rather loamy. From 23rd April until 5th May the rainfall was very heavy with over 4.36 inches falling in the period and between 18th April and 7th May the embankment on the Shapwick approach to the viaduct and abutment subsided 3½ inches. Since that date there had been further subsidence and on 23rd May the total subsidence was 30 ft at the north-east angle and 33 ft at the south-east angle. No. 1 pier had subsided 27 ft at the south end and 22 ft at the north end. Pain was of the opinion that if the subsidence continued at the present rate it would be necessary to remove Nos. 1 and 2 arches and to erect steel girders in their place. Had the subsidence not manifested itself the line would have been completed in time to open to traffic in early June.

As No. 3 arch was considerably weakened by the subsidence it was partially remedied by building the diaphragm walls in brick. On other parts of the viaduct where masonry had been damaged and concrete blocks crushed by the movement Marland bricks were set in cement mortar instead of concrete. Pain reported on 24th June, 1903 of another modification,

> Finding the subsidence of the embankment, abutment and No. 1 pier was gradually diminishing, I thought it desirable to put in two concrete struts from the base of No. 2 pier, so as to secure the latter against any injury due to the thrust of No. 1 arch and of the embankment above. This work has been done.

Erection of the viaduct spanning the Cannington valley, the major construction on the line, was aided by an aerial cableway across the valley. Built of concrete, the structure was 203 yards long with 10 elliptical concrete arches, with face blocks, each spanning a distance of 50 feet and supported on piers. The maximum drop from rail level to the valley floor was 93 ft (later officially stated at 79 ft 3 in.).

Although the greater part of the construction work was found completed, the intended opening date of Whitsun was cancelled. Because of the resultant delay the LSWR arranged for a horse-drawn bus to connect with trains at Axminster to run to Lyme Regis with fares 2s. 0d. inside and 1s. 6d. outside.

The summer months provided favourable weather for the final push to completion and arrangements were made for the official Board of Trade inspection, which was fixed for 21st August. Pain announced on 19th August, 1903 that all permanent way was laid and ballasted over the entire length of line. He then advised of outstanding work at Lyme Regis station where a short length of a goods siding required completing and ballasting. The widening out of the embankment opposite the station to form a coal stacking ground had yet to be finished and the contractor estimated a week to completion, the material having been brought from the trimming of the north slope of the cutting at Shapwick on the Axminster side of the viaduct. Minor additions were necessary in the engine shed, where the flooring required completion. None of the outstanding items interfered with the running of passenger services and as Directors, contractors and local dignitaries were keen for the line to open for traffic it was agreed the visit of the inspecting officer should proceed as planned.

Major E. Druitt conducted the official BoT inspection of the line on Friday 21st August, 1903 staying overnight at Lyme Regis and commenced his inspection at 10.00 am. Starting from Lyme Regis the special train was hauled by the two former London Brighton & South Coast Railway (LBSC) 0-6-0 'Terrier' tank locomotives, purchased especially for working the line. LSWR Nos. 734 and 735 in charge of drivers S. Dyer of Yeovil and W. Lailey of Exmouth Junction. The train formed of a saloon and bogie composite coach also conveyed J.R.C. Talbot, Mayor of Lyme Regis and one Director of the railway company, Mr Yerburgh, the contractor, A.C. Pain and Messrs Pain, Junior and A. Woodhill, representatives of the Engineer, as well as several representatives of the LSWR: Mr Holmes, chief operating superintendent from Waterloo, G.F. Valance representing the district superintendent Exeter, Mr Johnson, telegraph superintendent, Waterloo, Mr Annett, signal superintendent, Waterloo, Mr Granger, district engineer, Exeter, H. Higgs, district locomotive superintendent, Exeter, J. Curtis, permanent way inspector, Exeter and Mr Bulley, telegraph inspector Yeovil.

Several stops were made for examinations on the journey. Over an hour was spent inspecting the modifications to Cannington viaduct made after earth tipped against the Axminster end abutment had caused this and the No. 1 pier to settle and the intervening arch crown to rise. Druitt noted the arch crown had been replaced by a brick arch and diaphragm walls built to support the arch between Nos. 2 and 3 piers.

The inspector noted the line had been constructed under the Light Railway Order dated 1899. He found light railway No. 1 – 6 miles 4 furlongs and 5.60 chains in length and single throughout, connected on the up side of the LSWR station at Axminster and terminated in the Borough of Lyme Regis. Railway No. 2 was a short line for goods traffic only, 1 furlong 1.60 chains in length, running between the LSWR down goods siding and Railway No. 1 at a point about 3 furlongs 1 chain from its commencement and was not intended for passenger traffic and therefore no further reference would be made. Railway No. 1 was laid to a gauge of 4 ft 8½ in. with land sufficient for single line only. The width of the formation of the line was

LSWR notice of omnibus service Lyme Regis to Axminster 1st June, 1903.

View of Cannington viaduct from the west end during construction before No. 3 arch had developed signs of subsidence. The aerial cableway used during construction instead of scaffolding is evident. *Author's Collection*

'330' class 0-6-0 saddle tank No. 131 was used on the construction of the Lyme Regis Light Railway and proposals were mooted for members of the class to work the line after opening, a plan soon dismissed. Here sister locomotive No. 330 is shunting goods wagons.
Author's Collection

14 ft in cuttings and 16 ft on embankments with the steepest gradient 1 in 40 and the sharpest curve of 10 chains radius. The deepest cutting had a depth of 41 ft and the highest embankment was 55 ft. The fencing alongside the line was mostly formed of wrought iron standards and wire 4 ft in height; and the drainage was standard.

There were three stations on the line, including the LSWR station at Axminster, the others being Combpyne and Lyme Regis, the terminal. At Combpyne the single line platform was 260 ft in length, 15 ft wide and 3 ft above rail level, and a siding loop, the points being worked from a 4-lever ground frame with all levers in use, controlled by the keys on the single line Train Staff. Druitt also noted a booking office and shelter and retiring room for ladies had been provided a short distance from the platform. At Lyme Regis there was a single line platform 300 ft in length, 14 ft wide and 3 ft above rail level, with a booking office, general and ladies waiting room and retiring room. There was a run-round loop and sidings with an engine shed and goods shed. The connections to these were worked from a 5-lever ground frame with all levers in use, controlled by the single line Train Staff. At Axminster a new up bay line had been provided for trains from Lyme Regis to run into the back of the up main line platform with a loop for the engine to run round its train and a new connection between the up siding and the bay line. The Railway No. 2 joined Railway No. 1 by a connection facing to up trains, which was worked by a 2-lever ground frame with both levers in use controlled by the single line Train Staff for the line. The connection of Railway No. 2 with the down side LSWR siding was worked from a 2-lever ground frame, which was bolt locked from Axminster Station signal box. As a result of the alterations Axminster signal box now contained a 19-lever frame with all levers in use, of which two were of the push-and-pull type and one locked the Train Staff for controlling the points from the up LSWR siding to the new bay platform line. The interlocking and arrangements in the signal box and all ground frames was found satisfactory and correct.

In the course of the inspection Druitt noted there were five overbridges and 16 underbridges on the line. The overbridges had the necessary clearance and appeared to be standing well. Of the underbridges two were formed of cement concrete abutments with steel girders and corrugated steel flooring and one was of corrugated steel flooring supported on wooden trestles. Of the remaining underbridges 12 were formed of concrete arches and one of brick arch with concrete abutments. They all appeared to be standing well and the concrete to be of good quality and both girders and arches were found to have sufficient theoretical strength, the girders and flooring all gave very moderate deflections under test by the locomotives. There were nine arches of 3 feet or more in diameter under the line, all of which were of substantial construction and appeared to be standing well.

Although there were no tunnels or public road level crossings on the route Druitt spent a considerable time inspecting the principal feature on the new railway, Cannington viaduct. He found the structure was 182 yards in length (203 yards in official papers), consisting of 10 elliptical arches with spans of 50 ft each in the clear supported on piers, the greatest height being 93 feet (later officially quoted as 79 ft 3 in.) from the rail level to the valley below. The arches were formed of concrete in mass with facing blocks and the piers and abutments of concrete in mass, the bases of the piers and abutments being faced with flint. After the arches had been turned some settlement took place of the abutments at the Axminster end of the structure and No. 1 pier when the earth bank was tipped against the abutment, causing the crown of the arch between them to rise. The portion of the arch between the expansion joints was cut out in portions at a time and replaced by a brick arch and they had finally been

CONSTRUCTION AND OPENING

completed a month ago. The arch between No. 2 and No. 3 piers was also found to need support owing to settlement of the piers so the diaphragm walls were built and these to the time of the inspection had been effective. The abutments at the Lyme Regis end also settled slightly when the bank was brought up to it but no fracture occurred in either the abutment or any of the piers. The abutments were not visible at the time of inspection being covered by the earth slope. Druitt made a careful visual examination and found there was very slight vibration at the bottom of the piers when the two locomotives coupled together and carriages ran over it and as it was theoretically of sufficient strength and weight per square foot on the foundations he considered it safe for traffic. However, as a matter of precaution Druitt considered a watchman should be employed to note any serious settlement of a pier or abutment and that for the present the speed over the viaduct should not exceed 12 to 15 mph. It was agreed the watchman should be employed for an initial period of three years.

By view of its standing as a light railway the overall speed limit was restricted to 25 mph and the weight on any one axle to 12 tons. The only requirements stipulated by Druitt was the provision of a protective fencing at the wings of all the overbridges which the company engineer agreed to attend to at once. The removal of some temporary points near the viaduct and the connecting up of all facing points in the line to the rodding connecting them to the respective ground frames was required before the line opened to passenger traffic. Druitt also noted the view of an approaching train was very restricted at the occupational crossing near Great Trill Farm at 1 mile 40 chains and recommended the engine whistle be sounded for 200 yards before the approach to the crossing in each direction. The inspector noted the new railway was worked by one engine in steam in conjunction with the single line Train Staff and both the owning company and the LSWR, which was to work the line, had given the necessary undertaking as to its use; telephonic communication was established between stations. As the Axminster & Lyme Regis company wished to open the line for traffic on 24th August, Druitt sanctioned the opening of Railway No. 1 subject to the early completion of the outstanding requirements. After further stops the special arrived at Axminster just before 2.00 pm, when the LSWR personnel returned to Waterloo and Exeter.

As the decision was taken to open the railway the following Monday the jubilant Mayor of Lyme Regis called a special meeting of a committee of the town council to arrange the details for the official civic reception.

Monday 24th August, 1903 dawned fair after earlier heavy rain with showers threatening later in the day. Hastily erected flags and bunting was strung across thoroughfares in the town and the Union Jack was displayed over the parish church, where the bells were rung at intervals to celebrate the occasion. The Artillery band turned out to play selections of music and the whole town was *en fete*. The first train, the 9.40 am from Lyme Regis, was hauled by 'Terrier' 0-6-0Ts Nos. 734 and 735, which had worked up from Exmouth Junction where the crews had signed on at 4.00 am to prepare, decorate and work the engines for the great day. Four drivers were booked on duty, two acting as firemen. One pair were driver S. Dyer and driver G.F. Hawker acting as fireman. Watched by a large number of people the train departed from the flag-bedecked station without much celebration with 137 passengers on board, many of whom returned on the 10.45 am from Axminster. The official party included members of the town council, the Mayor J.R.C. Talbot with his scarlet robes, cocked hat and chain of office, members of Uplyme parish council, Mayor of Bridport councillor W.B. Northover, railway officials, representatives of the contractors and engineers and invited guests. The party assembled at the station at

The first train after arrival at Lyme Regis on 24th August, 1903 with the leading locomotive class 'A1' No. 734 adorned with flags, wreaths and garlands. The group posing for the photograph partially hide sister locomotive No. 735, which was running bunker-to-bunker with No. 734. The goods shed is in the right background.
Author's Collection

On the opening day and after the arrival of the train conveying VIPs the procession led by the mace bearer, mayor and clergymen make their way back to the centre of Lyme Regis.
Lyme Regis Museum

12.00 noon to travel by the second up departure of the day, the 12.25 pm ex-Lyme Regis and the 1.18 pm return from Axminster. For the schoolchildren of the area it was a half-day holiday and 200 lucky pupils made the return journey on the train for which they were issued special pink coloured tickets, 'their happy faces and merry voices' adding to the occasion. Subscriptions had been hastily solicited to pay the fare for the youngsters and to provide tea on the beach on their return. To convey such a large crowd totalling in all nearly 500 passengers, 13 gas-lit four-wheel carriages in the familiar salmon-pink livery including brake thirds, full thirds and composites each weighing 9 tons were provided and hauled by the two ex-LBSC 0-6-0Ts, the leading locomotive No. 735 decorated with flags on which rode Colonel Williams and Arthur Pain. For all services that day the pair worked bunker-to-bunker, No. 735 facing Axminster and No. 734 facing Lyme Regis.

Sharp to time at 12.25 pm, the train was heralded away by the newly-appointed station master Ley. Detonators were exploded as the train departed from the platform to the cheers of those left behind. The *Bridport News* for Friday 28th August, 1903 reported,

> The charming country through which the line passes is a joy to behold, Rhode Hill, the noble mansion of the Talbots, is seen standing out on the wooded slopes to the right on leaving the station, and then pretty little Uplyme peeps out from below, with its dainty villas and fresh green foliage, from the midst of which rises up the tower of the old parish church. All were impressed with the Cannington viaduct, a remarkably fine structure redounding to the skill of the engineer and the contractor alike. The gradient is very steep up to Combpyne and although the two engines were on, the speed at this point was very slow.

At Combpyne station master Greenslade was in attendance at the flag-bedecked station to watch the arrival and departure and 'rousing cheers greeted the train'. The *Bridport News* continued its discourse,

> From here to Axminster there is an incline, and in the course of the 6¾ miles, owing to the difficult nature of the country, there are several striking curves, which make the line all the more picturesque. All the way there is a succession of wooded hills, and magnificent stretches of fertile valley, making a series of panoramic views.

On arrival at Axminster the train was met by station master Ball, whilst the 'Pride of the Axe' band under the direction of bandmaster Fry lined up on the platform and played 'See the Conquering Hero Comes' as the train pulled in to the rousing cheers of spectators and afterwards 'Rule Britannia' and 'God Save the King'. The station was flag-bedecked for the occasion and members of the Axminster Parish Council welcomed the official party, who were joined by Sir John Kennaway Bart MP and other dignitaries. At the invitation of W.E. Pitfield Chapple, Chairman of Axminster Parish Council, the party proceeded to one of the waiting rooms on the down platform where champagne and other refreshments were served. Pitfield Chapple proposed a toast to the 'Success of the Axminster and Lyme Regis Light Railway', which was acknowledged by Colonel Williams, who was 'confident the line would be of immense benefit' to both towns. After the Mayor of Lyme Regis thanked the parish council for their cordial hospitality, the group rejoined the train.

On the return journey the 'Pride of the Axe' band rode on the train playing as best they could in the cramped conditions and during a halt at Combpyne station. The train's arrival at Lyme Regis was accompanied by exploding detonators and

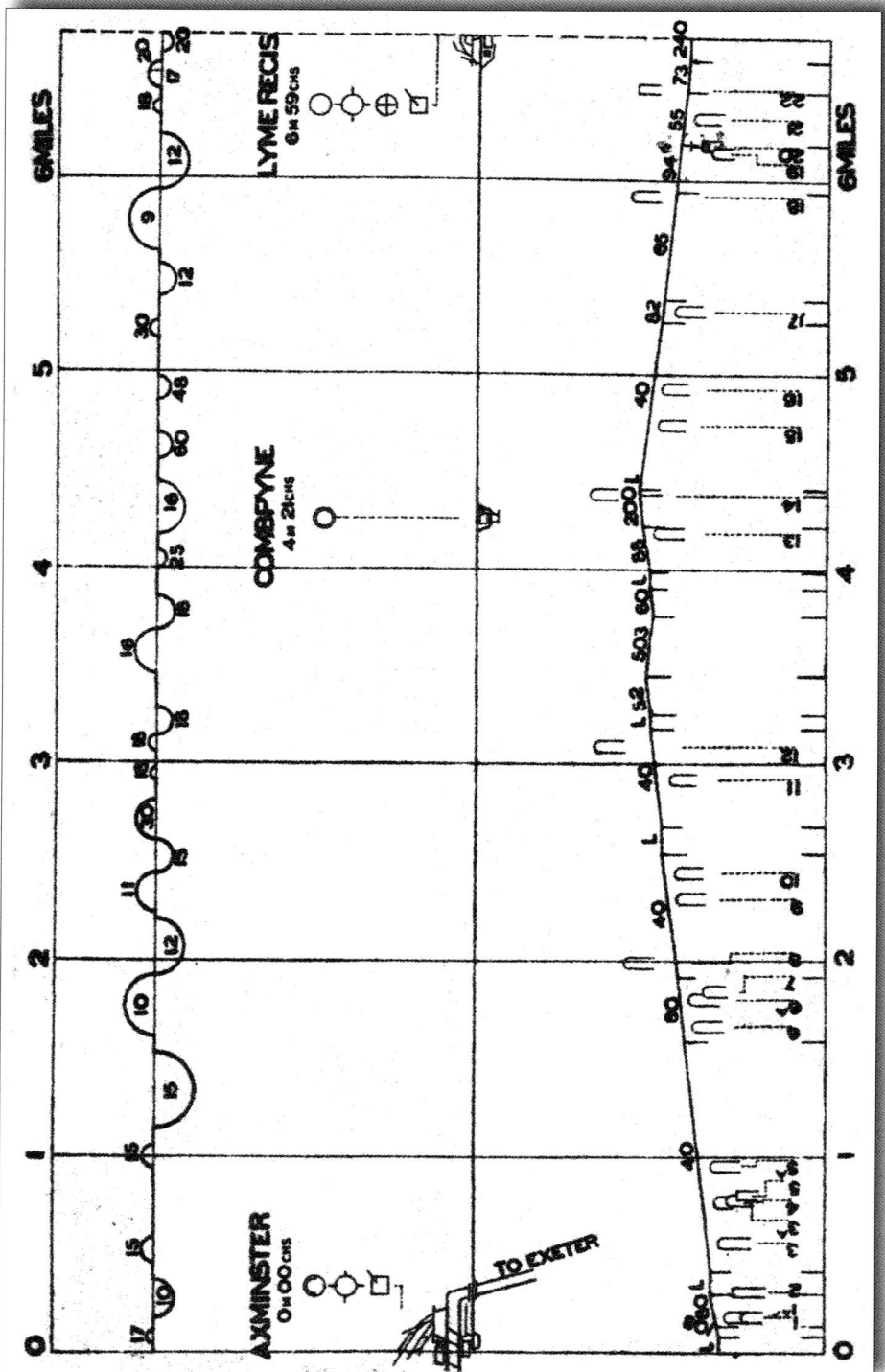

LSWR gradient and curvature chart, also showing the locations of the five overbridges and 16 underbridges.

spectators' cheers whilst the Lyme Artillery band, under the direction of buglemaster and conductor Fry, lined up on the platform and played a selection of melodies. Leaving the station a procession headed by the Axminster and Lyme Regis bands made for the town where the official party went to the Royal Lion Hotel for lunch, whilst the children were treated to tea on the beach.

The completion of the scheme and successful opening found the LSWR management expressing contrition:

> It was impossible to connect Lyme Regis with the railway system of the country without engineering works of considerable magnitude; but the facilities offered by the Light Railway Act and the skill of Mr Arthur C Pain, M.Inst.CE who has made a special study of this class of undertaking, have at last brought the expense of a line to Lyme Regis within practical limits.

At the time of opening the company Directors were Colonel Robert Williams MP of Brideshead, Dorchester, The Right Hon. Sir John Kennaway MP, H.H.J.W. Drummond of East Eudleigh, Devon, Frederic Julius Macauley of Alverstoke, North Side, Clapham Common, London SW and John Reginald Charles Talbot of Rhode Hill, Lyme Regis. H.G.S. Willams of 17 Victoria Street, London SW1 was Secretary and Messrs W.B. Pear & Co. solicitors.

The problems constructing Cannington viaduct had played havoc with the company finances and the final costs amounted to nearly £76,000, against the original estimate of £50,000 with the line costing £11,800 per mile. The LSWR was working the railway for 55 per cent of the gross receipts and could claim 4 per cent of the cost of any works undertaken on behalf of the Lyme Regis company. However, the main line company stipulated the light railway company was to finance any expenditure incurred making good any deficiencies which became apparent. After an official inspection conducted by the LSWR Engineer several items were cause for continuing concern:

> An underbridge at Uplyme, originally built of concrete, gave way during construction, in consequence of subsidence, and has been reconstructed with steel trough girders carried on timber supports. These timber supports must be considered as temporary works only, and when the time comes to replace the timbers with a permanent structure of masonry or concrete, the cost should fall upon the owning company. [His report continued that] at Lyme Regis the station buildings, goods shed and platform walls, being founded on a recently formed embankment, have of necessity been constructed in timber; these buildings must be regarded as temporary, and should be replaced hereafter by permanent structures in brickwork at a cost to the owning company.

Arthur Pain contested the LSWR claim:

> In regard to Walley Lane underbridge, I am of the opinion that it will cost less to maintain than if built of stone or concrete. I cannot therefore agree that the LSWR Company should not maintain it; the timbers should last for 25 years at least. The breastwork, if built of stone or concrete, would cost so large a sum that the interest on it would exceed the small cost of maintenance of the present structure.

Pain then commented on the concerns expressed regarding Lyme Regis and could not see why they were considered temporary, unless enlargement was necessary because of 'unexpected rapid development of Lyme', which was not considered imminent. He then questioned the demands of the LSWR management remarking, 'the LSWR Company have so many timber-built stations that I can hardly think they can ask the owning company to reconstruct them in say, 50 years hence'. He then said that in his opinion it would 'not be safe to build the goods shed or engine shed at any time in brick or stone, owing to the tender nature of the ground on which they stand.' The light railway company, however, conceded they would be responsible for any remedial work on Cannington viaduct for 12 months from the opening of the line.

The local press enthused,

> What marks an important epoch in the fate and history of Lyme Regis took place on Monday, in the opening of the Axminster and Lyme Regis Light Railway, which brings the delightful old town and the charming scenery of the neighbourhood into closer touch with the outside world. The fact is that it vastly increases the export and import carrying facilities, and makes the whole district easily accessible to visitors in search of a rest and recuperation by the sea.

At a company meeting held on 31st August, 1903 Colonel Williams reported to the gathering that 137 tickets had been issued for the first train from Axminster on the opening day whilst the second train carried 500. The remedial repairs to Cannington viaduct would cost an additional £1,500 to £2,000 while a supplemental agreement had been entered into, whereby the LSWR was afforded the opportunity of taking the whole of the light railway company's new issue of debenture stock.

Despite the euphoria the new railway was beset by troubles almost from the outset due to movement of the earthworks. Within a fortnight of the opening permanent way staff were checking the rails on the sharp curves as the track was spreading in excess of gauge despite the 'Terrier' 0-6-0Ts' relatively short wheelbase. However, with the opening of the line the private horse-drawn bus, operated by John Groves which had connected Lyme Regis with Axminster since the early 1880s and taken one hour on the journey, was withdrawn from the road, whilst seagoing freight handled on the Cobb declined rapidly. Of benefit to the town and railway was the establishment of the horse-drawn omnibus service connecting the Royal Lion Hotel in Broad Street and the centre of Lyme Regis with the station, obviating a long half-mile walk either up or down the steep hill. The buses, operated by Richard Harold Russell, departed from the hotel at 9.20 am, 12.10, 1.10, 2.03, 4.30, 5.55 and 7.15pm returning from the station at 11.01 am, 1.30, 3.30, 6.10 and 7.25 pm.

To accommodate the new railway a bay platform together with a water crane and primitive timber coal stage had been located at the back of the up main line platform at Axminster. However, on 7th October, 1903 the Lyme Regis Engineer reported that his LSWR counterpart wished to provide a 25 ft extension 'for the convenience of attaching goods trucks to the passenger trains' at an estimated cost of £9. The extension was on LSWR land and would be a convenience, not only to the Lyme Regis traffic, but also for unloading coal for the pumping engine, which formerly had to be done on the main line.' Authority was duly agreed. Further down the line the absence of a canopy on the exposed platform at Combpyne brought a request from a regular passenger for the provision of a short cover on the platform and a urinal. The LSWR management suggested the light railway company provide 'a small umbrella roof with seating' which would be appreciated by passengers, 'probably costing £50' but made no mention of the toilet facilities. The Lyme Regis company subsequently received a tender from Mr Caddy of Lyme Regis to complete the necessary work at a cost of £23 15s. 0d. but ultimately no shelter was provided. Yet further complaints were made on 7th October when a passenger 'appears to have complained on a wet day the urinal at Lyme Regis station was not covered in'. After investigation the work was completed by a Mr Irish for the princely sum of £5 5s. 0d.

Earnings on the light railway totalled £1,084 10s. 5d. from the opening until 31st December 1903, which both the Lyme Regis Directors and LSWR management considered satisfactory. Euphoria was short lived for in the winter months takings were negligible as many had travelled for the novelty of a train ride and had little intention of regularly using the railway.

The initial service of six mixed trains in each direction taking 25 minutes for the journey cut the previous coach times by half. On 17th May, 1904 the Lyme Regis company considered an application be made to the Light Railway Commissioner's before the end of the month for authority to increase the capital authorized in the 1899 order by £20,000, with borrowing powers for a further £8,000 by the issue of new ordinary and preference stock. The opening of the line which promised so much had never measured up to the expected success and the local company, faced with increasing financial difficulties, finally accepted the inevitable and sought a takeover by the LSWR. It was also evident to the A&LR and LSWR authorities that the 'one train only' method of working was considered a hindrance in the promotion for increased traffic levels and so arrangements were made to introduce Electric Tablet working of the single line with Combpyne becoming a train crossing point, thus increasing line capacity.

In 1904 a small goods storage hut was provided alongside the station building at Combpyne at a cost of £18 2s. 0d. after complaints were made that goods and parcels had to be left in the open under wagon sheets, but no further proposal was made for the erection of a urinal.

Major J.W. Pringle carried out the requisite BoT inspection of the branch improvements on 19th September, 1906 and found that the single line formerly worked by a single engine in steam carrying the Train Staff was now equipped for Electric Tablet working with the line divided into two sections, Axminster to Combpyne and Combpyne to Lyme Regis. The alterations and additions to signalling had been completed satisfactorily. At Axminster distant, home and starting signals for the branch along with ground signals had been provided and the existing signal box had been enlarged and the frame lengthened to accommodate the additional levers, which now had 30 levers all in use. Additional locking had been introduced with 'B' ground frame having two levers remaining and bolted from the signal box and 'A' ground frame with two levers, formerly controlled by a key on the Train Staff, now controlled by the Electric Token for the Axminster to Combpyne section. At Combpyne a new trailing connection had been installed from the loading bank siding with the up loop and the catch points on the up loop line had been removed so as to permit the station, with its island platform, to be used as a possible place for passing trains. A new signal box had been installed containing a 14-lever frame with 13 working and one spare lever, together with a new Tablet instrument. The signal box controlled distant, home and starting signals for each direction of travel and Pringle found the arrangements and interlocking satisfactory. Along the line at Lyme Regis the inspector found the position of some of the connections had been altered. The goods yard was now signalled for approach and departure and a goods shed was provided to protect freight traffic from the elements with access from one of the sidings. The new station signal box contained a 14-lever frame with all levers in use and the Tablet instrument for the Combpyne to Lyme Regis section of single line. The arrangements and interlocking were satisfactory.

Lyme Regis station in October 1903 with a 'Terrier' 0-6-0T at the head of a train of four- and six-wheel coaches, and a covered van. The original goods shed can be seen in the background and the cattle pen and loading dock in the foreground. *Author's Collection*

Lyme Regis station from the station approach road showing the northern extension of the station building erected for use as a W.H. Smith's bookstall but later as a store. A variety of bogie and six-wheel coaching stock form the train at the platform, whilst a passenger brake vehicle is stabled in the bay platform road. The entrance to the cattle pens and cattle dock has received gates to prevent animals from straying. A selection of horse-drawn vehicles waits for possible trade outside the station building. *Author's Collection*

Chapter Two

London & South Western Ownership

By Act of Parliament (8 Edw. VII cap. 85) which received the Royal Assent on 20th July, 1906 the LSWR duly obtained powers under agreements made on 4th April, 1900 and 19th May, 1903 to take the full assets of the Axminster and Lyme Regis Light Railway. This was duly arranged from 1st January, 1907 with the LSWR exchanging £55,000 Lyme Regis ordinary stock for LSWR 3½ per cent preference stock at par. At the time of takeover the authorized ordinary stock of £55,000 was fully paid up as was the £10,000 preference stock authorized in 1903. Of the £20,000 preference stock authorized in 1904, £5,000 remained unissued as did £6,000 of the authorized £20,000 debenture stock.

After less than encouraging receipts a geological upheaval occurred at Dowlands Cliff near Combpyne in January 1908 creating the phenomenon known as the 'Lyme Volcano', which resulted in a large upturn in the number of passengers travelling by train to view the scene. Debris from a cliff fall fell to the plateau below causing clouds of sulphurous smoke to be released. The debris contained bituminous shale, iron pyrites and cement stones and the effect of water on the pyrites and bituminous shale caused spontaneous combustion, which lasted for many months.

A casualty of the railway opening was the long-established horse-bus service connecting Axminster and Charmouth, which after losing trade was withdrawn from the road in 1911. Passengers preferred to travel by rail to Lyme Regis and then by the local horse-drawn omnibus, established in 1858, which served the popular tourist destination before continuing on to Bridport.

Such was the growth in interchange traffic at Axminster that complaints were made concerning the poor facilities on the up platform at the junction. The down platform was adequately covered by a canopy fronting the main station building but the up platform only possessed a timber waiting shelter to provide a refuge in inclement weather. In 1911 the LSWR authorities proposed to erect awnings along the entire length of the platform but, after investigation, it was found waiting times for passengers interchanging from the branch to main line services were minimal and as the cost of the scheme was estimated at £850, the expenditure was considered prohibitive and the plan was quietly aborted.

In the years leading to World War I the railway provided a much-needed opening for the expansion of freight in the area. Farmers and growers were keen to use the services offered by the railway company. The dispatch and receipt of livestock and other commodities, which had previously been hindered by the bad roads in the locality, was transported with ease. Meanwhile passenger traffic built up gradually, and tourist and excursion fares from Waterloo and other stations on the LSWR system supplemented local passenger receipts. By 1910 over 60,000 passengers were travelling between Axminster and Lyme Regis annually, coal and other merchandise imports to Combpyne and Lyme Regis exceeded 8,000 tons, whilst some 19,000 parcels were handled annually at the two stations.

After the encouraging news, disaster struck on the night of Friday 27th/Saturday 28th December, 1912 when the single-road timber engine shed at Lyme Regis, which could accommodate two locomotives, was destroyed by fire. Engine cleaner J. Short on night duty preparing the engine for the next day's work first noticed the outbreak

Lyme Regis station in the early years with 'O2' class 0-4-4T No. 184 waiting with her train at the platform. Although the Adams '415' class had taken over most of the branch services by 1913, the 'O2' locomotives, with tanks half-full to reduce weight, were used to cover in the event of maintenance or failure of the 4-4-2Ts. Note the Lyme Regis for Charmouth station nameboard and the incorrect route headcode carried by the locomotive. *Author's Collection*

An early view of Lyme Regis looking towards the buffer stops before the extensions were added to the station buildings. A LSWR 4-wheel brake third heads the stock stabled at the platform, probably a three-coach set as passengers wait to join the train. The goods shed in its original position is to the left. *Oakwood Collection*

An early view of Canrington viaduct with an 'O2' class 0-4-4T working an up train from Lyme Regis to Axminster. *Author's Collection*

about 4.10 am when he saw the roof engulfed in flames. As the building was constructed of pitch pine with a slate roof the fire rapidly spread. Short with admirable presence of mind climbed on to the footplate and manouvered the locomotive out of the shed and then raced to the town to summon members of the Victoria Fire Brigade and also driver-in-charge G. Hawkins. As the station was half a mile distant from the town the building was totally engulfed in flames before the fire brigade arrived. In the meantime station master C.H. Ley was one of the first on the scene and quickly realized nothing could save the structure. The firemen and other helpers were therefore directed to extinguish the flames and by 7.00 am the conflagration was under control leaving the shed as a few smouldering planks. A quantity of stores, including oil and personal effects of the footplate staff, perished. Damage was estimated at between £250 and £300 but the origins of the fire remained a mystery. The subsequent lack of facilities brought complaints from locomotive crews and a replacement was agreed as a matter of urgency. The new shed, constructed of asbestos-clad corrugated iron over a steel frame with accommodation for one engine, was completed on the site of the original structure the following year at a cost of £400.

After Germany declared war on France and Belgium, Britain declared war on Germany on 4th August, 1914 and, within days, volunteers for the armed forces were departing from Lyme Regis, Combpyne and Axminster. The departures by train were proud but sad occasions as some did not return. On the outbreak of World War I, the LSWR with other British railway companies came under Government control from the same date, under the powers of Section 16 of the Regulation of the Forces Act 1871 with the Railway Executive Committee taking control under the chairmanship of Herbert Walker, later Sir Herbert Walker of the LSWR. The Lyme Regis branch services initially continued to run to pre-war timetables, but the issue of all excursion and cheap day tickets was suspended and all competition between companies cancelled. Goods traffic increased as additional produce from local farms was sent to towns and cities to make up for the loss of imported goods. Even hay was cut from railway embankments and sent to military stables. Some local railwaymen answered the call to arms and joined the colours in the first few months of hostilities. Not all was bad news for in 1915 there was a boom in first class travel on the LSWR as travellers, who usually migrated to France or Switzerland, took holidays at South Coast resorts including Lyme Regis.

A unidentified 'O2' class 0-4-4T climbs through Combpyne Woods with a 6-coach train of four wheel stock. Note the original 56 lb. per yard flat-bottom track. *Author's Collection*

Combpyne station with an unidentified Adams Radial tank locomotive departing with an Axminster to Lyme Regis train. The view taken in the late 1920s shows the signal box at the south-east end of the platform and the former up loop, where the platform facia and edging are still extant, occupied by open wagons. A connection off the back siding, also occupied by an open wagon, served the short dock road with the associated cattle pens. By this date all internal points in the goods yard were hand operated. *Oakwood Collection*

Despite the increase in traffic most train movements between the main line and the branch at Axminster were performed via the up side transfer siding, and the short 840 ft spur connecting the down main line via the goods yard was rarely utilized, only occasional freight movements removing the rust from the rails. Being for a greater part on a rising 1 in 40 gradient and a left-hand curve of 10 chains radius, the spur proved an operational inconvenience. The track and connections were subsequently removed on Sunday 5th September, 1915, when possession of the line could be achieved with minimum inconvenience.

By December 1916 the strain of the war effort was taxing the resources of all British railways to such an extent that the Railway Executive issued an ultimatum that they could only continue if drastic reductions were made to ordinary and non-essential services. The Lloyd George Coalition Government agreed to a general reduction in passenger services from 1st January, 1917, but with these economies the Lyme Regis branch lost only one train in each direction as some services operated as mixed trains conveying goods as well as passengers. Thus the branch continued its useful activity giving regular passenger, freight and parcels services to the local community. In the same month further evidence of railway encouragement to local people came after the German 'sink at sight' submarine campaign threatened imports of food and near starvation. Allotment holders, including those encouraged to rent plots alongside the branch, were urged to increase the cultivation of vegetable and fruit. Second class railway travel was abolished on 22nd February, 1918 and the coaching stock downgraded to third class - over the years improvements had been made to third class interiors so there was little difference in quality of accommodation.

Traffic declined slightly during World War I due to the withdrawal of excursion traffic, but after the cessation of hostilities they were resumed in 1919. The general feeling of elation felt by the armistice in November 1918 was shattered by a railway strike, which halted branch services from 26th September to 5th October, 1919. During the war railwaymen received a war bonus for working under difficult conditions but the 1s. 0d. to 1s 6d. per week was to be withdrawn from 1st January, 1920 and the grievance was sorely felt by the staff. The action undermined the patronage enjoyed by the railway as prospective passengers sought alternative modes of transport. The following year the first signs of competition came on 2nd February when a motor bus service was introduced by Butler Brothers between Bridport and Axminster station via Charmouth, running initially twice weekly and then four days a week from May 1920. Although not in direct competition with the Lyme Regis branch the new service quickly succeeded in removing most of the Charmouth traffic from the railway. In addition farmers and growers realized for the first time that with improving roads, goods could be conveyed by lorry, using in some cases vehicles purchased second-hand from the military; thus short journeys to local markets were possible at cheaper rates than charged by the LSWR. The door-to-door services were more convenient than double handling into and out of railway wagons. The primitive road vehicles of the day were not, however, capable of continuous long hauls and long distance traffic remained safely in the hands of the railway company.

A few years after the removal of the down side connection at Axminster the LSWR goods manager reported the early abolition of the facility had proved embarrassing as the goods exchanging to and from the Lyme Regis branch required shunting across the main lines and resulted in delay to services. Thus in 1921 the company contemplated the reinstallation of the connection but when the cost was estimated at

£1,335 the matter was dropped. It was then proposed to provide two sidings on the same site, one with capacity for eight wagons, but again costs proved prohibitive at £746 and the scheme was abandoned; the LSWR at this period was suffering from post-World War I financial difficulties. Economies were, however, made at Combpyne in the same year when all signal arms were removed leaving only the points to the loop operated from the signal box.

With the early success of road transport other bus proprietors soon extended their territory and the inevitable happened on 8th July, 1922 when the National Omnibus and Transport Co. introduced a service between Axminster station and Lyme Regis continuing on to serve Charmouth, Bridport and West Bay, operating four journeys in each direction on weekdays and three each way on Sundays. Despite the poor roads in the area a shorter and more direct contact was provided between the villages and hamlets and the two towns, with fares between Axminster and Lyme Regis of 1s. 0d. single and 1s. 9d. return and between Axminster and West Bay of 2s. 6d. single and 4s. 0d. return. Little concern was felt at the time but the service was the birth of the cancerous growth which four decades later finally destroyed the branch line. Although peace had been declared the Government retained control of the railways until 15th August, 1921 as the war effort had seriously debilitated the concerns with little or minimal maintenance of rolling stock and infrastructure. In 1918 the Coalition Government had hinted at support for nationalization, a thought that had been festering since the formation of the Railway Nationalisation League in 1895 and with later support of the railway unions and the formation of the Railway Nationalisation Society in 1908. A number of industrialists and traders were sympathetic saying the railways should be a public corporation rather than a profit making concern. The *Railway Gazette* in 1919 even proposed nationalization. In the event the Government fell short of full nationalization and formed the over-100 individual companies into four groups. The impending Grouping of the railways meant the problem of road competition was of little concern to the LSWR management in their last months of administration.

Lyme Regis station in 1903 with 'Terrier' tank locomotive No. 735 standing at the platform with a train composed of two brake thirds and a composite. The terminus, located 249 ft above sea level and half a mile from the town , is in original condition with ballast and shingle between timber retaining walls. The track is the original flat bottom weighing 56 lb. per yard in 30 ft lengths and the ballast is a mixture of chalk and gravel. The cattle loading dock is to the right. *Author's Collection*

Chapter Three

Southern Railway Operation

As a result of the Railways Act of 1921 the LSWR was absorbed into the Southern Railway and from 1st January, 1923 the Lyme Regis branch came into its third ownership. Under the new aegis the existing frequency of services was initially maintained and excursion traffic increased, whilst through coaches from Waterloo to Lyme Regis were introduced on summer Saturdays.

The new management made few initial changes to the branch but as the months passed the LSWR livery on the locomotives gave way to Southern Railway green whilst the coaching stock followed suit. The company officers soon took stock of the new assets and quickly realized the difficulties faced by passengers changing trains at Axminster. A proposal was mooted in 1923 for the ornate platform buildings on the down side to be abolished and replaced by a new modern structure straddling the main lines with access from the widened Western Road overbridge, whilst at the same time increasing the platform faces from three to four with the Lyme Regis branch having direct access to and from the main line. Costs, however, were considered prohibitive when it was realised the interchange of traffic was only at its maximum for about 12 weeks of the year.

Industrial action then affected affairs and a seven-day railway strike from 20th January, 1924 brought a decline in traffic. The deteriorating relationship between trades unions and the railway company only served to encourage competition and gradually bus services offering door-to-door transport increased. The affairs of the branch were again disrupted by the General Strike in early May 1926. Railway union members withdrew their labour in support of the miners and subsequently train services could not be guaranteed, and on several days the Lyme Regis branch services were suspended. Fortunately within a week regular railwaymen returned to duty and services resumed. The impact of the continuing miners' strike meant reduced coal stocks available to the railway companies and the SR authorities decided to conserve stocks by reducing train services for a short period.

In the late 1920s the Southern Railway attempted to nullify bus competition by acquiring shares in the Southern National Omnibus Company, which itself had acquired the local bus services in the area. During subsequent years an integrated transport policy was followed with buses covering the early morning Lyme Regis to Axminster and the late evening Axminster to Lyme Regis services. The timings were shown in the railway timetables as connecting with main line services; winter Sunday services were also covered by the bus company. By this expediency the SR made considerable savings in manpower costs as the wages of station staff and train crews could be brought within two shifts with minimal extra overtime. The Southern Railway regularly publicized the line and the area with attractive posters depicting the Cobb at Lyme with fishermen on the east wall. The popularity of country walking and rambles together with Sunday League and other excursions did much to sway the SR to introduce a regular Sunday service of 12 trains in each direction during the summer months from 1930. However, the long climb from the town to the terminus was a source of annoyance to many but connecting road transport continued to be provided and by the early 1930s George E. Halliday was the proprietor of the local bus service, which met all trains at Lyme Regis station. The same year saw the SR reaching agreement with the unions for the withdrawal of

'415' class 4-4-2T No. 0520 has just arrived at Lyme Regis with the branch train from Axminster on a soggy 26th August, 1928. *H.C. Casserley*

SR 'D1' class 0-4-2T No. B359 standing at the head of the 1.18 pm branch train to Lyme Regis at Axminster on Sunday 4th May, 1930. Four of the class suitably modified with reduced coal and water capacity were sent to work on the branch from 1929 as replacements for the Radial tank engines but they quickly proved unsatisfactory and the 4-4-2Ts were reinstated.

H.C. Casserley

'D1' class 0-4-2T No. B359 stands at the head of a branch train at Lyme Regis on 4th May, 1930. Note the cutdown bunker required to allow the class to run on the light railway and the ornate lining on the paintwork.
H.C. Casserley

Adams '415' class 4-4-2T No. 3520 in immaculate Southern green livery and fitted with a Drummond boiler reflects the sun as she runs round her train at Lyme Regis in the early 1930s.
Oakwood Collection

The branch train in the bay platform at Axminster on 21st May, 1935 with No. 3520 awaiting departure. Note in the background the tall chimney of the boiler house whose steam engine pumped water from the River Axe to the tank top. *H.C. Casserley*

Taking water at Axminster; '415' class No. 3520 standing at the end of the bay platform on 25th May, 1935. *H.C. Casserley*

guards from passenger services on various branch lines where the trains were formed of three coaches or less. Initially this was only considered for branches operated by push-pull operation but ultimately included the Lyme Regis branch. The instruction was on the understanding that the train was composed of vehicles fitted with the vacuum brake throughout, or fully-braked and piped-only vehicles in the proportion authorized in the regulations for working the vacuum brake. Two fully-braked four-wheel freight vehicles could be conveyed in place of one passenger carrying vehicle. The working without a guard required the station master or other authorized person to carry out the duties stipulated in rules 129 (iv) and 141 (b). In the event of a train being stopped by accident or other exceptional circumstance, the driver had to satisfy himself that all was in order to proceed in accordance with rule 141 (e).*

As well as increasing traffic a critical investigation into the economies of the branch soon revealed the crossing loop at Combpyne was rarely utilized and could effectively be removed without inconveniencing the operation of train services. Although the loop had been little used since installation it was necessary to retain a siding for goods traffic, and as the majority of freight traffic was incoming it was decided to remove the points at the Axminster end of the loop so that wagons could be dropped off or collected by down goods or mixed trains. As a result of these economies the signal box, north-end points for the up loop and associated signalling were abolished from 17th June, 1930. The platform was also refurbished and concrete walls provided as the facing to the main single line. At the same time the station master's position was withdrawn leaving the station staffed by a leading porter. The station master at Lyme Regis duly assumed authority for the entire branch exclusive of station limits at Axminster. At this period the platform at Lyme Regis was extended, the entire length being provided with concrete walls and facings to cope with the 6-coach through services to and from Waterloo on Summer Saturdays.

Just prior to the outbreak of World War II, on 1st September, 1939 the SR with all other railway companies came under the control of the Railway Executive Committee. Within weeks of the commencement of hostilities local bus services were reduced and from October 1940 winter Sunday train services were reintroduced and then maintained throughout the hostilities. Part of the wartime activities to combat the threat of invasion was the removal of station and signal box nameboards. 'Lyme Regis for Charmouth' and 'Combpyne for The Landslip' nameboards disappeared but after the war when replacements were erected the new boards bore no reference to Charmouth or The Landslip. Posts and other obstacles on station platforms received white stripes of paint to obviate people walking into them in the dark or blackout. The agricultural nature of freight handled on the branch was again of the utmost importance as vital provisions of home-grown food, grain and vegetables were dispatched and conveyed to local markets.

In 1938 the bay platform at Axminster was widened necessitating the realignment of the Lyme Regis branch permanent way and repositioning of signals but the work was not officially inspected until 19th June, 1945 when the inspector noted the bay platform serving the Lyme Regis branch had been widened and the permanent way adjusted and aligned with rails weighing 95 lb. per yard. The signals had been repositioned to suit the altered alignment and to cope with the additional facilities four new levers had been installed in the existing signal box.

---

* Rule 129 (iv) related to checking the train was properly formed and equipped; Rule 141 (b) covered starting the train by use of a green flag or light; in the case of Rule 141 (e) there was no longer a guard for the driver to liaise with.

'415' class No. 3520 standing alongside Lyme Regis engine shed on 31st August, 1945 in the SR black livery. Note the large stack of coal on the stage and the water column used for replenishing the locomotives. *H.C. Casserley*

Axminster station, 144 miles 65 chains from London Waterloo, facing towards Yeovil from the down platform in 1948. '415' class No. 3125 occupies the up main line near Western Road overbridge No. 444, whilst covered footbridge No. 444A connecting the up and down platforms is in the foreground. *Author's Collection*

After the war the railways resumed peacetime activities with run-down and life-expired rolling stock, equipment and infrastructure in need of maintenance. Questions were raised in Parliament regarding the deteriorating services offered and the Lyme Regis branch was no exception. In 1945 as one of the 4-4-2Ts was hauling the single-coach 12.33 pm Axminster to Lyme Regis train the locomotive was partially derailed approaching Combpyne after colliding with a tractor, which had run through the fence and down the embankment. The tractor had moved of its own accord, out of gear on a falling gradient with the farmer in close pursuit. The engine suffered a broken steam pipe and damage to the firebox but fortunately the brake composite carriage remained on the rails. Services were disrupted until the Exmouth Junction breakdown gang arrived to re-rail the engine using jacks and old sleepers. A replacement engine was then sent to work the line as the re-railed engine was sent back to Exmouth Junction shed for examination. In 1946 the SR attempted to revive tourist and holiday traffic as families took the opportunity to take their first post-war holidays. Many services were crowded with day-trippers as well as those spending a week by the sea, despite fares rising by 16 per cent from pre-war levels. At this period the Southern Railway was busily engaged in building Bulleid-designed 'West Country' class 4-6-2 tender locomotives for main line passenger and mixed traffic work and it was the practice for the naming ceremony to be enacted by a local dignitary at the station at or rear the place named. In August 1946 No. 21C109 was named *Lyme Regis*, but as the class was prohibited by weight from the branch, the naming ceremony took place at Axminster station when Alderman H. Blanchard, who was mayor of Lyme Regis and a member of the station staff, performed the ceremony.

The severe weather early in 1947 brought problems, initially with snow blocking the cuttings and then rapidly thawing snow causing minor flooding to the permanent way. Waterlogged sleepers had to be replaced and ballast re-distributed under the rails. This was not the only problem for, as petrol rationing eased, so Southern National improved the frequency of the local bus services. Further progress was hampered by a critical shortage of locomotive coal supplies and the government announced at the end of April 1947 that to conserve stocks for the following winter, train services were to be cut by 16 per cent compared with the summer of 1946. On a brighter note in 1947 as part of the routine painting and maintenance programme Lyme Regis station received much-needed attention. The station buildings were extended, receiving new timber cladding and a new roof. At the same time the engine shed was refurbished and repainted.

Camping coaches first appeared in Britain in the summer of 1933 when the London & North Eastern Railway (LNER) introduced a number at holiday resorts in East Anglia and the North East. The London, Midland & Scottish Railway (LMS) and GWR followed from the summer of 1934 but the Southern did not introduce their first camping coaches, known as 'bungalows on wheels', until 1935 when 12 vehicles were installed for the summer season at eight different sites in Hampshire, Devon and Cornwall. By 1939 this had expanded to 17 different sites including Kent and Sussex but during the war years the coaches were commandeered for strategic purposes. In 1947 the coaches were re-introduced when Combpyne was one of the nominated sites. The first coach provided was a converted former London, Chatham & Dover Railway six-wheel vehicle.

As the railways were still under Government control and it was the declared intention of the Labour Government to nationalize the majority of public utilities and associated industries, including railways, which they had announced in their 1945 election manifesto, the scene was set for further changes to the Devon/Dorset branch railway.

The settlement of the piers on Cannington viaduct was fairly even but the settlement of the west abutment and first pier was greater than elsewhere and crushed the crown of the first arch. To counteract this movement two diaphragm walls were built in brickwork in cement in the third span, to enable it to act as an abutment and concrete needles were built in the embankment between the first and second piers, the crushed portion of the first arch was cut out and made good in brickwork and parapets over this arch completed. The remedial work in the third arch is evident in this view of an unidentified Radial tank crossing the structure on an up train.

Ivo Peters

Crossing one of the many concrete covered brick underbridges on the branch Radial tank No. 30583 heads her single-coach train towards Axminster. *Author's Collection*

Chapter Four

Nationalization and Closure

The 1947 Transport Act of 6th August brought the amalgamation of the Southern Railway Co. into the nationalized British Railways from 1st January, 1948 and the Lyme Regis branch came under its fourth ownership, that of British Railways, Southern Region.

On 1st January, 1949, temporary lengthman S. Marchant sustained fatal injuries when run down by a train, whilst working on the track near Lyme Regis. The subsequent Ministry of Transport inquiry was conducted by J.L.M. Moore who learned that the train in question was running as a special, without previous notice and was formed of a class '415' class 4-4-2 tank locomotive running bunker first hauling a 20 ton goods brake van. George William Johns, the driver was on the left side of the footplate in the direction of travel, but did not see Marchant on the track although he approached him round a 14 chains radius left-hand curve. Moore found there was a particularly good range of vision through the square windows over the bunker of this class of engine, and Johns himself admitted that as the coal did not obstruct his view he could hardly have failed to see Marchant had he been looking out. He stated that he had occasion to notch up the reversing lever a second time after leaving Lyme Regis, and as this involved turning his back momentarily on the direction of travel it probably explained why he failed to see the man on the track. Johns' first intimation of the accident was the application of the hand brake by the guard, who caught sight of the man in front of the engine when looking through the left-side window of his van, and then saw him lying in the four foot after the train had passed.

Moore was of the opinion that it was unfortunate that Johns chose that particular moment to attend to the reversing lever as he was traversing a particularly bad portion of the line, from the point of view of visibility, and had noticed men at work there when passing in the opposite direction a few minutes earlier. The driver should also have taken into account the fact that he was working an unscheduled train, for which men on the track might be unprepared, and therefore made a point of keeping himself free to look out, at any rate until he was safely past the men he had seen. Had he done so he would have had nearly 100 yards view of Marchant and as the train was travelling at only 10 to 12 mph, the accident might have been avoided.

The inspecting officer was of the opinion the primary responsibility for the accident rested upon the deceased, as the guard was definite he was standing on the track with his back to the train and his two companions shared the same view, though with less certainty. It was strange Marchant was in that position as the hut where the men started work, and where a pair of gloves was later found, was towards Lyme Regis. In conclusion Moore could only suggest that on reaching the track the deceased either paused whilst trying to recollect where he had last laid the gloves, or was looking for them on the ground. His lapse was surprising as his eight years working on the single line branch should have left him in no doubt as to the need to be constantly on the alert from traffic from either direction, especially at the site of the accident where visibility was particularly bad.

The branch featured in the film *All Over The Town* released in 1949 and starring Sarah Churchill, Cyril Cusack, Norman Wooland and Bryan Forbes. A gentle black

Lyme Regis station from the buffer stops with '415' class No. 30584 running round her train on 7th July, 1959. Through coaches for the service to Waterloo are berthed in the bay platform.
H.C. Casserley

'415' class No. 30582 runs round her single-coach train at Axminster on the evening of 10th July, 1960. Axminster signal box of typical LSWR vintage, which controlled all points and signals at the junction, can be seen at the country end of the down main line platform.
R.C. Riley

comedy on provincial politics the film commenced with 4-4-2T No. 3125 arriving at Lyme Regis and showed a later view of the stationary locomotive.

Few alterations to the timetable were made under nationalization until 1951 when a coal crisis forced the cancellation of Sunday trains from 14th January until 1st April. Despite formal protests by the Lyme Regis Borough Council and individuals, winter Sunday services were curtailed thereafter never to return and from then on Southern National buses again maintained connections.

Holiday traffic increased during the early 1950s bringing much needed revenue to the line but increased car ownership and the inconveniently sited stations did much to relieve the line of local passenger traffic. Southern National buses provided an almost door-to-door service for those reliant on public transport and many winter trains ran almost empty. Summer services were reasonably full and holiday runabout tickets and cheap day return tickets helped to popularize the line.

The British Transport Commission had, however, requested Regions to investigate the viability of lines which had fluctuating amounts of traffic between summer and winter and the Southern Region chief accountant submitted a report on the Lyme Regis branch to his General Manager on 12th June, 1952.

> If the branch were closed, I assume there would be no loss of local and through parcels and freight receipts. The traffic presumably, would be collected and delivered from Axminster instead of Lyme Regis, albeit at some extra cartage costs. [He continued] Apart from those passengers travelling on the Summer only through coaches to and from Waterloo, the great majority of passengers already have to change at Axminster and, indeed the timetable indicates that on certain services the passengers travel between Axminster and Lyme Regis by Southern National Omnibuses when no suitable train is available on the branch. In my opinion, therefore, if this branch were closed most of the passengers would continue to travel by rail to Axminster, and there should be little loss of passenger revenue apart from the earnings arising on travel local to the branch, which would be small. The Southern National Omnibus Company (which is wholly owned by the British Transport Commission) would obtain additional receipts which might, or might not, cover their additional costs, but broadly speaking it does appear if this line were closed an increase in British Transport Commission net revenue of, say, roundly £15,000 per annum would be effected.

The commercial superintendent begged to differ and considered that the Lyme Regis branch was remunerative but added a rider that it 'might not continue as such'.

On Sunday 28th June, 1953 as part of their 25th anniversary the Railway Correspondence & Travel Society ran a special train from Waterloo to Lyme Regis and then on to Exeter. A former LSWR 'T9' class 4-4-0 tender locomotive hauled the train from Waterloo to Axminster in 2 hours 49 minutes including a stop for water at Salisbury, arriving at 12.34 pm where a special four-coach train was waiting in the bay platform to take the participants on to the coastal resort. The branch train was double-headed by 'Ǝ15' class 4-4-2T No. 30583 piloting 'A1X' class 0-6-0T No. 32662. The surviving ex-LSWR representative No. 734, which had become No. 32646 was requested but had failed and so No. 32662 deputized. Station master W.H. Mairs met the train on arrival from London and octogenarian G.F. Hawker, a former member of the footplate staff at Lyme Regis, was invited on to the footplate of the 'Terrier' tank to renew old acquaintances before the train departed. No. 32662 allocated to Fratton shed had arrived earlier and ran trials over the branch on 10th June.

From the 1954 summer season the camping coach at Combpyne was a converted former LSWR bogie non-corridor composite coach, which except for sojourns at

What appears to be super power on the Lyme Regis service at Axminster is in fact change over day for the Radial tanks working the branch. No. 30582 taking water has been replaced by sister locomotive No. 30584 waiting to depart with her one coach 'BCK' as the next train to the coast. After departure of the service No. 30582 will make her way to Exmouth Junction shed for maintenance and boiler washout.

Author's Collection

'415' class No. 30582 pulling into the exposed platform at Combpyne, 4 miles 21 chains from Axminster, with a down train as the porter waits with platform barrow to assist any passengers alighting. In the background the camping coach occupies the end of the goods siding.

Author's Collection

The 10.35 am special train to Lyme Regis climbing the 1 in 80 out of Axminster on 27th June, 1959. The pair of '415' class Nos. 30583 and 30582 are hauling six London Midland Region vehicles to form the return holiday special for the Boys Brigade from Lyme Regis to Oldham.

S.C. Nash

Radial tanks Nos. 30584 and 30583 forge up the 1 in 40 gradient near Combpyne with a down train conveying through coaches from Waterloo in 1960.

Ivo Peters

Additional power for the through coaches from Waterloo to Lyme Regis. '415' class 4-4-2Ts No. 30584 with 'lion and wheel' emblem on the side tanks (leading) and No. 30583 pound up the 1 in 40 gradient towards Combpyne with the 4.36 pm train from Axminster on a Saturday in June 1960. The train has just passed under Hartsgrove overbridge No. 12 at 3 miles 07 chains .
Ivo Peters

'415' class No. 30583, having uncoupled from her train, drifts towards the end of the platform at Lyme Regis prior to running round the coaching stock to form the return working to Axminster.
Oakwood Collection

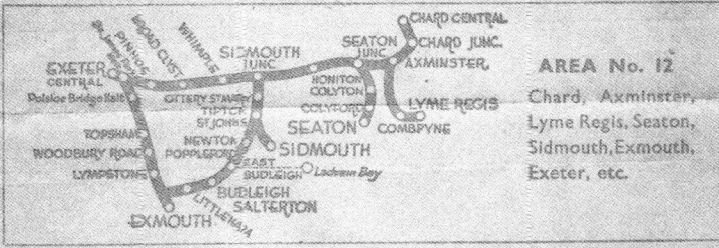
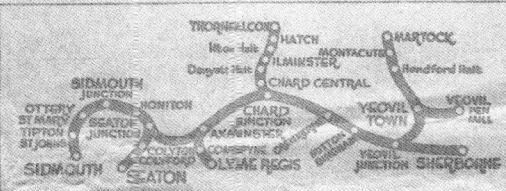
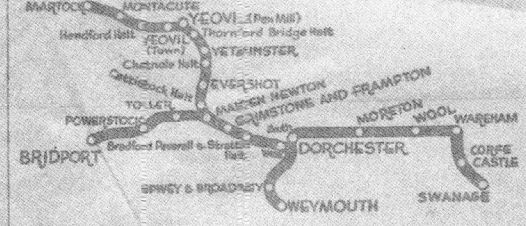

Holiday Runabout Ticket pamphlet showing the two areas incorporating the Lyme Regis branch.

Ivatt LMR '2MT' 2-6-2T No. 41306 heads away from Axminster with her single-coach train to Lyme Regis. *Author's Collection*

LMR '2MT' 2-6-2T No. 41309 standing in the sunshine at Lyme Regis with two-coach set No. 109 forming the branch train for Axminster. The bay platform is to the right. *Author's Collection*

Eastleigh during the winter months served at the intermediate station until the final season in 1963.

The Gloucestershire Railway Society organized a railtour of West Country lines on 10th May, 1958 utilizing a three-car cross-country dmu. The special ran from Cheltenham St James departing 9.10 am via Gloucester Eastgate, Bath Green Park and the Somerset & Dorset line to Templecombe before visiting the Lyme Regis branch. The return departed at 4.19 pm and ran by way of Yeovil, Frome, Radstock and the North Somerset line. The fare was £2 2s. 6d. with a surcharge of 7s. 6d. for those passengers upgrading to first class.

In August 1958 the branch stations had issued 2,500 tickets and collected approximately 8,000 monthly but in winter months the figure dropped to approximately 1,500 issued and collected.

On rare occasions special trains were worked through to Lyme Regis and typical was the 6-coach formation of former LMS or BR (London Midland Region) stock bringing the Oldham Boys' Brigade for their annual camp on 20th June, 1959. The train required the use of two of the '415' class 4-4-2Ts and after the passengers had alighted and their luggage removed the six vehicles were shunted into the back siding and stabled, there to be cleaned and washed before being worked away, until required for the return journey on 27th June. The return journey was double-headed by 4-4-2Ts Nos. 30582 and 30583. At Axminster the train was taken over by 'T9' class 4-4-0 No. 30719 for the onward journey. The stabling of such trains often caused problems at Lyme Regis for it reduced the siding space for goods traffic. In the same year No. 30583 suffered a shifting tyre on one of the driving wheels when crossing Cannington viaduct but was able to reach Lyme Regis before being declared a total failure. A bus provided a covering service for passengers until a replacement engine was sent from Exmouth Junction. The failed engine was later hauled dead at a slow pace back to the Exeter shed for repairs.

The long reign of the Adams 4-4-2Ts on the branch came to an end in 1961 when after trials and alterations to the permanent way LMR class '2MT' 2-6-2Ts took over all services.

Despite the possible threat of closure the Southern Region *Holiday Haunts* booklet for 1962 extolled the excellence of the area:

> Lyme Regis, a pleasant little all-season resort on the Dorset-Devon border, sheltered from the north and east winds, has glorious golden sands, perfectly safe for bathing at all times, with hundreds of pools at low tide to delight the young yachtsmen and shrimpers. The harbour shielded by the famous Cobb, is filled in summer with yachts and boats of all kinds, and many trips can be made from it to neighbouring ports. It is a favourite spot for artists. There are good fishing, sailing and rowing, with many aquatic events. There are also first-class facilities for bowls, tennis, golf and cricket, and good entertainment at the Marine Theatre, Regent Cinema and Woodmead Dance Halls. The interesting museum contains much to delight the geologist. The Langmoor Gardens are delightfully laid out. [It concluded] There are many walks through the superb scenery along the coast or inland to some of the charming old-world villages of Dorset, Devon and Somerset.

Axminster also received a mention:

> It is now a pleasant little market town, whose only link with the past is its church, which has a Norman doorway, but is chiefly Perpendicular. Set in a dairy-farming countryside, of great charm and interest, it has walks and drives to such delightful villages as Kilmington, Colyton, Colyford and Rousden. There are good views from the ancient

The Gloucestershire Railway Society tour of West Country lines from Cheltenham St James on 10th May, 1958 utilized a Western Region three-car Cross-Country diesel-multiple-unit for the journey which included the Somerset & Dorset route before terminating at Lyme Regis. Here the unit stands at the branch terminus before departing on the return working at 4.19 pm.
Oakwood Collection

Lyme Regis on the occasion of the visit of the Gloucestershire Railway Society tour to the branch on 10th May, 1958. The Western Region three-car Cross-Country diesel-multiple-unit complete with headboard stands at the platform as participants inspect the station and goods yard.
Oakwood Collection

LMR '2MT' class No. 41206 standing at Lyme Regis with the LCGB 'East Devon Railtour' train on 28th February, 1965, with sister locomotive No. 41291 at the rear. By this date the run-round loop was still in position but the points clipped out of use, whilst the track in the goods yard had been removed leaving the goods shed isolated. *Author*

LMR '2MT' No. 41291 standing hard by the buffer stops at Lyme Regis after hauling the 5-coach LCGB 'East Devon Railtour' train from Axminster on 28th February, 1965. Sister engine No. 41206 stands at the other end of the train ready to lead the way back to the junction. The same locomotives hauled a repeat of the tour on 7th March, 1965 but with only three coaches.
Author

The afternoon of the last day of passenger services finds a three-car diesel-multiple-unit standing in the late autumn sunshine in the bay platform at Axminster before forming the next departure to Lyme Regis. *Brian Jackson*

Lyme Regis station buildings in July 1976 surviving well a decade after the closure of the line, with prolific growth of buddleia encroaching. The building was dismantled in 1979 and now serves in a resurrected capacity at Alresford on the 'Watercress Line'. *Brian Jackson*

earthworks of Membury, Musbury and Lambert's Castle, and the ruins of Newenham Abbey, founded in 1246, are in the near neighbourhood.

The harsh winter weather, which commenced on Boxing Day 1962 and continued almost continually until the following March badly affected railway services and the branch suffered from the snow and icy conditions. On several days when a blizzard was forecast, the branch locomotive, an Ivatt '2MTT', was kept in steam overnight to operate across the branch to keep the line open, although on at least two occasions snow blocked cuttings near Combpyne. In the intervening period the branch was transferred from Southern Region to Western Region administration from 1st January, 1963, and local railwaymen expected considerable changes.

The Beeching Report published in 1963, advocated closure of the branch and quoted the following figures:

Passengers	0 to 5,000 per week
Freight traffic	0 to 5,000 tons per week

Combpyne dealt with £0 to £5,000 traffic per annum and Lyme Regis £5,000 to £25,000 traffic per annum.

Through summer services remained during the 1963 timetable and regular steam traction finished with the advent of the diesel multiple units to the branch on 4th November, 1963. On the same day Combpyne became an unstaffed halt. With the new traction the running time between Axminster and Lyme Regis was reduced from 21 to 18 minutes, an average of 22½ mph, but still within the 25 mph limit imposed by the Light Railway regulations.

The branch remained intact during 1963 but on 3rd February, 1964 freight facilities were withdrawn from both Combpyne and Lyme Regis. At the end of August notice was given of the intention to withdraw all branch passenger services on and from 30th November, 1964. Loud protests were made, action groups formed, and the formal objections were duly made at a Transport Users' Consultative Meeting held at Lyme Regis on 4th November. Whilst the outcome was awaited, minor economies were made and the single line Tablet operation was replaced by 'one engine in steam' working. During this period the Locomotive Club of Great Britain twice visited the branch when their East Devon rail tour trains ran across the line on 28th February and 7th March, 1965. On the first occasion the five-coach train was hauled by two LMR 2-6-2Ts, No. 41206 at the Axminster end and No. 41291, at the Lyme Regis end of the formation but the second train was limited to three coaches with the same engines. In the intervening period, on 5th March, No. 41216 became derailed at Lyme Regis and sister engine No. 41223 was sent to assist and after the rerailing to work the branch services.

After a prolonged wait caused by difficulties in arranging additional bus services the Minister of Transport announced on 9th September, 1965 his decision to allow the withdrawal of services. The decision caused disappointment but despite eleventh hour attempts to stave off closure, the traffic commissioner issued the necessary bus licences and the closure date was fixed on and from 29th November, 1965.

On the final day of operation, Saturday 27th November, local people and railway enthusiasts mingled to ride on the last trains. At Lyme Regis flashlight photographs were taken before the last up train driven by Tom Woodman departed at 7.10 pm over exploding detonators into the darkness to negotiate the sharp curves and

During 1974 an ambitious scheme was launched to reopen part of the branch near Combpyne. Work commenced on the 1 ft 3 in. gauge Axe & Lyme Valleys Light Railway and rolling stock was acquired from the Longleat Railway in Wiltshire. By 1976 construction had ceased and in this view facing Combpyne station on 8th July, 1976 the track is overgrown and rolling stock abandoned. *Brian Jackson*

View of the abandoned Axe & Lyme Valleys Light Railway looking towards the cutting at Combpyne on 8th July, 1976. The rolling stock was dispersed for use on other light railways.
Brian Jackson

NATIONALIZATION AND CLOSURE

Cannington viaduct on its way to Combpyne. More cheering, waving and singing greeted the departure of the diesel multiple unit at 7.17 pm from the lonely wayside station and soon the train was carefully negotiating the falling gradients to Axminster. On arrival at the junction at 7.28, again to exploding detonators, passengers were quickly detrained and the unit dispatched empty to Exeter; thus the 62 years life of the line expired. Civic parties from both ends of the line had travelled on the last train, some in period costume and enjoyed a formal tea at Axminster before the final round trip, which had departed the junction at 6.48 pm.

The track soon disappeared under a carpet of weeds and undergrowth, and small saplings sprang up between the sleepers in Combpyne Woods. Axminster signal box was abolished on and from 5th March, 1967, whilst the contract for the removal of the track of the closed branch was arranged in late 1966 and by April 1967 dismantling had commenced at Lyme Regis working slowly back towards Axminster. For some of this work the contractor utilized a small 0-4-0 diesel mechanical locomotive built by John Fowler in 1940 (Works No. 22920) bearing the grandiose name of *Risley Yard No. 111 MED*. This was transferred to site from the Ministry of Defence Naval Dockyard at Portland and once work was completed in 1967 it migrated to Birds Commercial Motors Ltd, Long Marston, Warwickshire. The gradually deteriorating station building at Lyme Regis was finally sold to the Mid Hants Railway for use at Alresford and dismantled early in 1979.

In 1974 an ambitious scheme was instigated, under the title of The Axe and Lyme Valleys Light Railway, installing a 1 ft 3 in. narrow gauge line on the trackbed of the branch at the former Combpyne station. Around three-quarters of a mile of track was laid and rolling stock acquired from the Longleat Railway in Wiltshire in November 1974 and January 1975. In addition to 13 coaches two steam engines and six diesel locomotives were transferred to the embryonic line. Because of financial and other difficulties construction was never completed and the project was terminated in 1976. The steam locomotives included *Lyme* an outside-cylinder 0-6-0 built by Berwyn in 1967, transferred to the Lappa Valley Railway, Cornwall in May 1976 and *Axe* an outside-cylinder 0-6-2T built by Severn-Lamb Ltd which returned to Longleat in April 1975. Diesel-mechanical locomotives included *The Cub* built by Minirail in 1954 and sent to J. Critchley, Birnbeck Pier Railway, Weston-super-Mare in October 1976; *Pooh* built by R.A. Lister dating from 1942 and transferred to the Lappa Valley Railway, Cornwall in June 1975; *Zebedee* built by R.A. Lister in 1938 which went to the Paradise Railway, Hayle, Cornwall in May 1975 and an unnamed, unnumbered machine new to the line and built by Minirail in 1976 subsequently transferred to the Dudley Zoo Railway in October 1976. The two diesel-electric locomotives were *Doctor Diesel* built by Minirail and Severn-Lamb in 1969, which went to the Blenheim Palace Railway, Woodstock, Oxfordshire in October 1976, and D2 *AmberArrow* built by Minirail *circa* 1960 sent to the Lappa Valley Railway, Cornwall in July 1976.

Today the overgrown trackbed of the erstwhile Axminster & Lyme Regis Light Railway can be followed for most of the way and is easily discernible hugging the hillside. In a few places local landowners have taken over the formation to extend their property but memories of this line will linger with faint echoes of the Adams 4-4-2Ts tackling the steep gradients at a sedate pace.

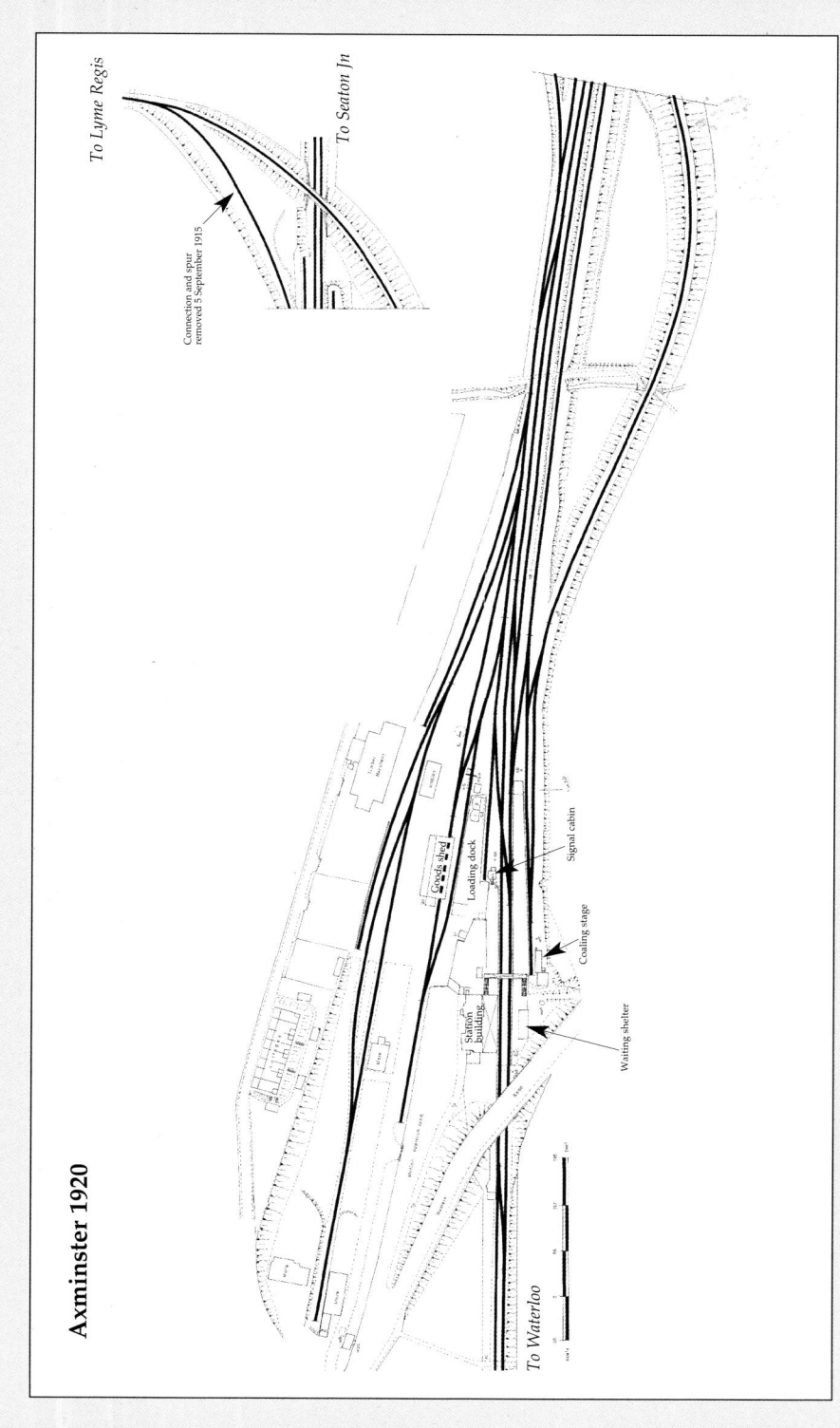

Chapter Five

The Route Described

Axminster is a pleasant market town in the county of Devon situated on a slope above the River Axe, famed for its association with the carpet industry, which died in 1835 but was revived in the early 20th century. The station designed by Sir William Tite opened on 19th July, 1860, lying to the south-west of the town centre and 144 miles 65 chains from London Waterloo on the former LSWR main line to Exeter, had up and down main line platforms and a bay at the west end of the up platform, which was used by the Lyme Regis branch trains. The main station buildings, booking office and waiting rooms were located on the down platform, with the signal box sited at the base of the west end ramp. The up platform boasted a waiting shelter only, the wooden structure originally walk through but when the SR installed a new water column on the platform, doors were provided at each end and the open centre section was boarded up to prevent passengers from possible injury or soaking. Spanning the line was Western Road overbridge No. 444 whilst the platforms were connected by covered footbridge No. 444A. In the early years of the Yeovil to Exeter main line a small engine shed was located on the down side of the line to house the locomotive used to assist westbound trains on the ascent of Honiton bank, when '460' class 4-4-0 Nos. 0460 and 0472 were recorded on such duties. By 1896 it had fallen into disuse and was demolished when the station layout was remodelled in anticipation of the Lyme Regis branch. The main line followed a straight course through the platforms before following 104 and then 120 chain radius right-hand curves passing the goods yard on the down side and goods reception line on the up side.

Lyme Regis branch facilities included a run-round loop located mostly out of the platform, and by the buffer stops, a water tower, water column and coaling stage used to replenish the branch locomotive. On 7th October, 1903 six weeks after the opening of the branch Arthur Pain reported,

> ... the LSWR Engineer has asked that the branch platform road at Axminster shall be extended 25 feet for the convenience of attaching goods trucks to the passenger trains at the estimated cost of £9 0s. 0d. This extension is on LSWR Company's land and would be a convenience, not only to Lyme Regis traffic but also for unloading coal for the pumping engine, which formerly had to be done on the main line.

The water was pumped from the adjacent River Axe, the pump house having a tall brick chimney. Drivers were warned that at certain times a truck of coal could be stabled on the up bay line opposite the coal stage and they were to exercise care when entering the station under these conditions.

A connection off the main branch line, immediately in advance of the starting signal at the end of the platform, led to an interchange siding with the up main line. Actual transfer could only be achieved by a reversing movement, for the points from this siding formed a trailing connection with the up main line. This up reception siding was used to transfer through coaches to and from the branch as well as to set up main line freight trains back to clear the main line for faster passenger services.

The arrangements for handling the branch services required careful planning; on the arrival of a train from Lyme Regis, the engine and passenger coaches ran into the

The ornate Axminster station in the years before the building of the Axminster & Lyme Regis Light Railway. The approach to the station from the town by way of Western Road was wedged between the LSWR main line and the goods yard. Two Bradford & Sons Ltd of Yeovil open wagons occupy the siding in the foreground serving the coal grounds, whilst in the background on the siding nearest the station entrance are three cattle trucks and an assortment of private owner and LSWR open wagons. Note the simple waiting shelter on the up platform, the tall up starting signal and the absence of the tall water tower which later dominated the scene.
Oakwood Collection

Axminster station viewed from the road approach, with a selection of horse-drawn vehicles including a horse bus awaiting the arrival of a train. The ornate building designed by Sir William Tite with prominent gables and large chimney stacks, features shared with others on the line including neighbouring Honiton, was located on the down platform and opened for traffic on 19th July, 1860. Facilities included station master's accommodation, booking office, booking hall, waiting rooms and staff rooms.
Oakwood Collection

Axminster station facing east from the up platform in 1960. The signal box and down starting signal are to the right and the Lyme Regis bay platform to the left. The open wagon by the buffer stops in the bay platform has been used to bring locomotive coal supplies to the coaling stage.
Author's Collection

A view looking west from the down main platform at Axminster with covered station footbridge No. 444A spanning the up and down main lines and the Lyme Regis branch bay platform at the rear of the up main platform. The water tower and tank are to the right.
Oakwood Collection

'415' class No. 30584 standing by the buffer stops in the bay platform at Axminster in October 1957, with the water column and small coaling platform to the left. Note the front of the footplate below the smokebox door has a collection of oil lamps behind the route headcode disc.

Author

Adams '415' class 4-4-2T No. 30582 taking water in the bay platform at Axminster. The locomotive is in the early BR lined livery with lion and wheel emblem on the side tanks.

Author's Collection

Road side aspect of the large goods shed at Axminster erected by the LSWR in 1860. The goods office at the eastern end of the building replaced a small cramped office located within the structure. *A.E. West*

Goods shed at Axminster showing the loading platform within the structure. *A.E. West*

LMR '2MT' class 2-6-2T No. 41322 leaving Axminster for Lyme Regis with a branch service. The single branch curves away to the right with the parallel run-round loop. To the left the trailing connection from the up main line leads to the up reception siding which was used to transfer goods and passenger traffic between the branch and the main line. *Author's Collection*

An up branch train headed by '415' class No. 3520 negotiating the curve on the approach to Axminster on 31st August, 1945. The train is about to cross bridge No. 2 over the main line at 0 miles 25 chains from the junction. *H.C. Casserley*

up bay platform. However, to permit the engine to run-round its train the stock was then propelled clear of the points to the run-round loop. After running round, the engine backed on to the coaches so new passengers could join the train for the return working to Lyme Regis. Occasionally some passengers joined the train by entering the rear vehicle standing in the platform and enjoyed a 'free ride' as the engine backed the stock into the platform. Through coaches for Waterloo were detached from the branch set and placed in the up reception siding to await the arrival of the up main line train. In the down direction through coaches from Waterloo were detached from the main line service in the down platform before the branch engine backed on to the stock. The formation was taken forward and then backed over the crossover to the up main line. Here the engine took the stock forward into the up reception siding before backing into the bay platform and on to the branch stock. The second engine if required and especially on summer Saturdays then backed on the head of the train, which was doubled headed to Lyme Regis.

The Lyme Regis single line served the straight branch platform 280 ft in length and 80 ft above sea level. From the platform the single branch swung right on a 17 chain curve climbing at 1 in 108 and then left on 10 chain radius curve climbing at 1 in 80 to cross the up and down main lines by an iron girder bridge No. 2 (also numbered 444C on the main line) 17 ft 6 in. above track level and 25 chains from the station. The space between the curvature of the branch and the main line was utilized for the storage of permanent way equipment and for many years the tender from locomotive No 0470 was stabled in the yard to serve as a water storage tank. Halfway between the platform and the bridge on the down side was a brick anti-aircraft gun pillbox installed in World War II. Immediately after crossing the bridge on the level the former connection from the down goods yard climbing at 1 in 40 to meet the branch, made a trailing connection on the down side. This short section shown in the Parliamentary plans as Railway No. 2 was controlled from two 2-lever ground frames – that connecting off the siding in the down side goods yard was bolt locked from Axminster signal box whilst the connection with the branch was locked and released by a key on the single line Tablet. The connection was removed on 5th September, 1915.

After the short level section the line continued in a southerly direction climbing at 1 in 40 on a short 15 chain radius right-hand curve and then straight, and at the three-quarter mile post the main Axminster to Seaton road, the A358 Fosse Way, was crossed by an underbridge No. 4 at Abbey Gate (also known as Abbey Lane), 0 miles 62 chains. Just to the north of the bridge the Axminster up fixed distant signal was located as the railway continued climbing on a shelf of the hillside where broad panoramas of the Axe valley were to be seen to the west.

Between milepost 1 and milepost 2 the railway continued climbing at 1 in 40 negotiating a 15 chains radius right-hand curve before swinging east on a long 15 chains radius left-hand curve A short straight section in a shallow cutting led to another 10 chain right-hand curve passing over a culvert and a farm track at Trill, where the engine whistle had to be sounded for 200 yards when approaching from either direction. The line then negotiated a 10 chains radius right-hand curve where the gradient eased to 1 in 80 before climbing again at 1 in 40 on a 12 chains left-hand curve before passing under Collier's occupational bridge near milepost 2. Still climbing at 1 in 40 the 12 chains radius left-hand curve continued followed by a 11 chains right-hand curve as the branch headed east through a shallow cutting. The sinuous nature of the branch continued with 15 chain left-hand and 30 chain right-hand curves as the line veered south past Park Farm, on an 18 chain right-hand

Combpyne 1912

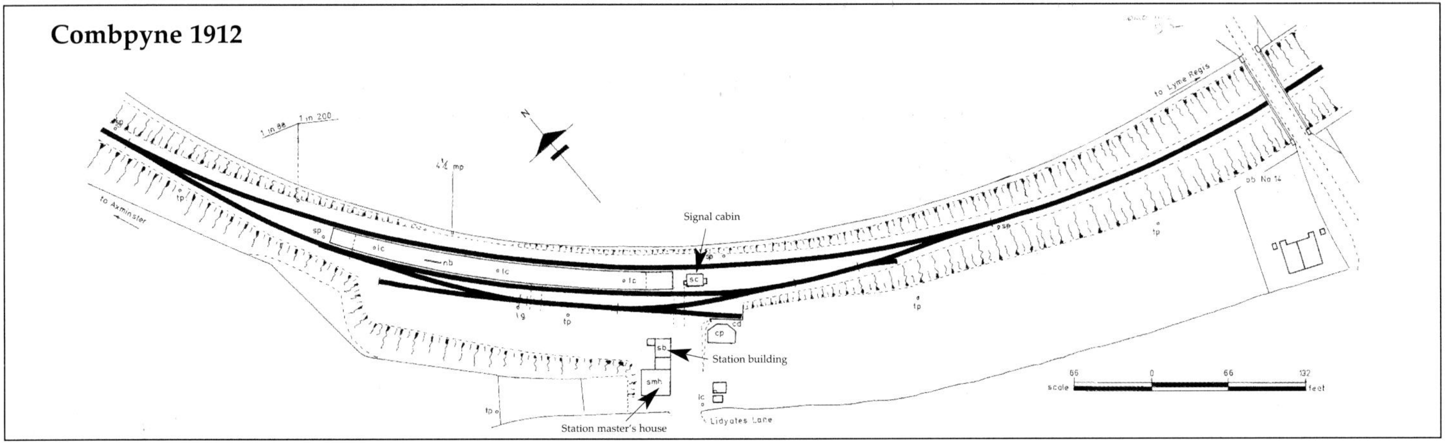

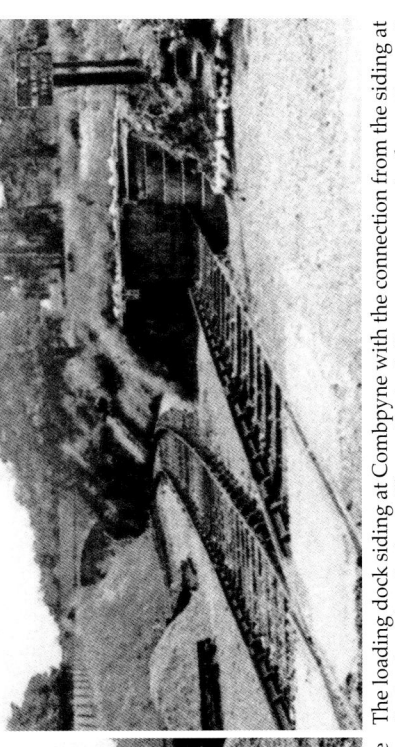

Combpyne station 4 miles 21 chains from Axminster in 1903 showing the original flat-bottom track weighing 56 lb. per yard in 30 ft lengths laid on a ballast of broken stone and gravel. This was soon found inadequate and was replaced by heavier rail. A variety of wagons occupy the loop line and sidings.

The loading dock siding at Combpyne with the connection from the siding at the back of the platform. The main single line curves away in the cutting and under overbridge No. 14 towards the summit of the line at 476 ft above sea level.

A.E. West Author's Collection

curve before straightening out through wooded countryside near Hartsgrove farm, where an occupational overbridge spanned the line at 3 miles 07 chains.

Still hugging the hillside the railway levelled out near the 3¼ milepost where an 18 chain left-hand curve was negotiated followed by a straight section climbing at 1 in 52. A falling gradient of 1 in 503 on a 16 chains right-hand curve was followed by a 16 chains left-hand bend as the line resumed climbing at 1 in 60. The light railway skirted Shapwick Hill passing through Combpyne Woods with its oak, hazel and beech trees and bluebells and primroses carpeting the ground in season. Approaching milepost 4 a short level section was followed by a climb at 1 in 88 as the line passed Combpyne Hill on a 25 chains radius left-hand curve bearing east over Combpyne Farm occupational underbridge No. 13 to enter the exposed Combpyne station, 4 miles 21 chains from Axminster, known in the initial years as Combpyne for the Landslip and located on a 16 chains left-hand curve. The nameboard was removed in the early 1940s because of the threat of invasion and when restored was plain Combpyne. The *Bridport News* reporter enthused on 28th August, 1903 'from Combpyne, the panorama is grand; Seaton Down, Beer Head, the mouth of the Axe, and the silver streak of the English Channel are to be seen'.

The station located some three-quarters of a mile from the hamlet it was supposed to serve at a height of 470 ft above sea level originally possessed an island platform 260 ft in length with up and down loop lines passing either side, but when the up loop was converted to a siding the edging stones on that side were removed. The platform 3 ft in height was devoid of shelter for passengers and the brick-built station building was situated south of the line adjacent to the lane leading to Rousdon and Higher Bruckland. This contained the living accommodation for the station master and his family, and later leading porter, whilst alongside was a single-storey building containing a booking office, waiting room and ladies' and gentlemen's toilets, a luxury for such a remote location.

The timber signal box opened, in 1906, which had a 14-lever frame was located immediately off the east end of the platform ramp but when this was removed in 1930 the ground frame occupied a site adjacent to the points leading to the siding and south of the line. The signal box, similar in design to that at Lyme Regis was subsequently removed and served as a store and later chicken coop on a local farm. In the reorganization the platform was modernized by the provision of new concrete facings provided from Exmouth Junction concrete works. Platform lighting was by two oil lamps but before closure Tilley lamps were utilized, being suspended from the lamp standards at each end of the platform.

During the later years on the branch when freight traffic was in decline the siding at Combpyne was occupied from 1947 by a railway camping coach in the summer season. As there was no mains water supply, water was sent up from Lyme Regis in five gallon churns by the first up train and delivered to the occupants by the porter-in-charge, empties being returned to the terminus by the first down working. The Combpyne porter was also responsible for ordering replacement bed linen and other items for those using the camping coach, soiled linen being placed in hampers and sent for laundering with a new hamper containing fresh linen being received in return. Great hopes for development of the station were made in the early years as one report stated: 'At present there is scarcely any population hereabouts except at Rousden, the beautiful cliff estate of Sir Wilfred Peek; but there is excellent scope for the development of accommodation for visitors, the site being an ideal one for the erection of a hydropathic establishment or residential hotel'. Needless to say nothing transpired and the station stayed in a somnolent state for its complete existence.

Combpyne station facing towards Axminster after the improvements made in 1930 incorporating concrete platform fascia and edging. The siding at the back of the platform had a connection to a headshunt serving the loading and cattle dock seen on the left.
Author's Collection

Combpyne station house and station office framed by the loading gauge spanning the siding at the back of the platform in 1955. *A.E. West*

Combpyne for the Landslip station 4 miles 21 chains from Axminster facing towards Lyme Regis with the 260 ft single platform on the up side of the line in the late 1930s after the abolition of the signalling and conversion of the passing loop into a siding running at the back of the platform. The reference to 'the Landslip' referred to the tourist attraction at the nearby Dowlands Cliffs.
Author's Collection

The building containing the booking office and waiting room at Combpyne in August 1958.
A.E. West

A four-coach down train double-headed by '415' class No. 30583 and 'A1X' class 0-6-0 'Terrier' tank No. 32662 enters Combpyne station on the 10th June, 1953. The trial run was being made in connection with an RCTS special train, which ran with four coaches later in the month on Sunday 28th June. The train is passing the original camping coach to be allocated to the station, former London Chatham & Dover Railway six-wheel vehicle, numbered S1 in the camping coach fleet, which served at the remote station during the summer months from 1947 until replaced in the autumn of 1953.
Oakwood Collection

A holidaymaker watches from the window of the camping coach as Radial tank locomotive No. 30584 with blower on and steam shut off slows to a halt at Combpyne with the two-coach 12.33 pm train from Axminster on 8th September, 1958. Note the concrete edging to the platform.
H.B. Priestley

After a brief rise at 1 in 200 on the 16 chains left-hand curve out of Combpyne to the summit of the line, 476 ft above sea level, as the branch entered a cutting before passing under New Road overbridge No. 14 at 4 miles 31 chains. Leaving the cutting the line descended at 1 in 40 following a straight course across an embankment and then over Shapwick occupational underbridge No. 15 on a 60 chains left-hand curve. Shapwick Grange Farm lay in the valley on the up or right-hand side of the line before the railway entered another shallow cutting negotiating a 48 chains left-hand curve before the gradient eased to 1 in 82 falling over Cannington viaduct. With a maximum height of 93 ft (later stated as 79 ft 3 in.) above valley level and the lowest arch 53 ft in height the viaduct was the major engineering feature of the branch. Magnificent views of the valley could be seen from the train as it crossed the 203 yds-long 10-arch structure, whilst in the valley below stood the former Combpyne signal box now used as a farm outbuilding. The construction of the concrete viaduct received coverage in *The Railway Engineer* in 1905:

> The viaduct in question is situated at Cannington, on the Axminster and Lyme Regis Light Railway, which now connects Lyme Regis with the Yeovil and Exeter line of the London and South Western Railway. It consists of ten elliptical arches of 50 feet span, its total length being 600 feet, width over spandrels 16 feet, maximum height to rail level 92 feet and gradient of 1 in 80. It affords an example of the recent application of concrete to viaduct construction and to arches of somewhat large span. With the exception of the concrete blocks in the vertical faces of the arches, the work throughout is mass concrete.
>
> The geological strata are greensand and blue lias clay. The foundations, originally designed for a pressure of 3½ tons per square foot, were enlarged to give pressures ranging from 1½ tons to 3 tons per square foot. The concrete used consisted of crushed flints and Portland cement, the crushing yield insufficient grit to make the addition of sand unnecessary except in special cases. The concrete was hand mixed, and for transporting this and other materials a cableway of 1,000 feet span was erected across the valley, the piers being built without scaffolding.
>
> The piers were carried up in rectangular lifts of diminishing size, instead of having a continuous batter, the lifts being 6 feet deep. The concrete was deposited in wooden boxes of this depth, which were bolted up on the ground and hoisted into position. The mode of filling and striking the boxes, of which there are eleven, is described. The work in all the piers was advanced as far as possible at the same rate.
>
> Two rows of corbels were built in the top lift of the piers to support the arch-centring. This consisted of four built ribs, the centre portion of which was tied by a framework, in the form of a Warren girder, supported in the middle by taking struts from the lower row of corbels. The ribs, including the lattice-work, were set in one piece, and four tie-bolts were placed in the span to assist the piers in taking the thrust.
>
> The faces of the arches were built in concrete blocks, of which two similar ones on opposite sides of the viaduct were set simultaneously by a rail attachment to the cableway; by adjusting the chains attaching the blocks the latter suspended at the angles required by their position in the arch. The blocks were keyed in advance of the mass concrete, in order that the adhesion of the latter to the toothing of the blocks might relieve the centres of some of the weight.
>
> Expansion joints were formed through the arches, spandrels and parapets, and are found effective in giving play for expansion and contraction and any slight movement due to settlement. In turning to arches, the centring, although apparently light, was found to be sufficiently rigid, and the setting was facilitated by the ribs being made in one piece.
>
> The settlement of the piers was for the most part fairly even, and being adjusted as the work proceeded, did not affect the concrete; but the settlement of the west abutment and

The completed Cannington viaduct from the Lyme Regis end and with the jack arch in place under the defective third arch. Note the four-rail timber fencing erected alongside railway property. *Author's Collection*

'415' class Nos. 30582 and 30584 cross Cannington viaduct with a 5-coach train on 12th September, 1959, including through coaches from London worked to Axminster on the 10.45 am Waterloo to Seaton train. The branch working departed the junction at 1.50 pm arriving at Lyme Regis at 2.11 pm. *Ivo Peters*

first pier was greater than elsewhere, and crushed the crown of the first arch. Two diaphragm walls were built in the brickwork in cement in the third span, to enable it to act as an abutment, and concrete needles were built in the embankment between the first and second piers; the crushed portion of the first arch was cut out and made good in brickwork, and the parapets over this arch were completed. Particulars are given of the cost of the viaduct, and a schedule is appended of the results of tests of sample blocks made from materials used in the concrete.

The authors believe this is the first instance in which piers of a similar height have been built without scaffolding, and in which the centres of a 50 foot arch have been designed for setting in one piece.

Leaving the viaduct the branch swung in a northerly direction on a 12 chains left-hand curve descending at 1 in 65 along an embankment and past Cuckoo Hill before sweeping into a cutting. Away from the cutting the line then swung to the east on a sharp 9 chains right-hand curve across an embankment giving views of the village of Uplyme and the countryside beyond. Approaching milepost 6 the line again passed through a cutting 23 ft in depth where a small overbridge, No. 18 at 5 miles 73 chains, carried the lane to Hook Farm across the line. Falling at 1 in 94 Lyme Regis fixed distant signal was then passed as the railway followed a 12 chains left-hand curve skirting the hill close to Uplyme before following a short straight section and then turning on a 18 chains radius right-hand curve in a southerly direction. Another cutting supported by concrete breastwork was entered as the branch passed underneath the main Axminster to Lyme Regis road, near the Black Dog Inn, which formed the Devon-Dorset county boundary by Lyme Road overbridge No. 22 at 6 miles 37 chains. Dipping at 1 in 55 and 1 in 73 the line passed the Lyme Regis up advance starting signal by the 6½ milepost and then the down home signal, engine shed and coaling stage on the down side of the line as the gradient eased before entering Lyme Regis station, 6 miles 59 chains from Axminster on a 1 in 240 falling gradient. Prior to World War II the station nameboard had announced 'Lyme Regis for Charmouth', overlooked by Colway Cottage. After hostilities the pre-stressed concrete nameboard carried 'Lyme Regis' on metal sheeting.

Situated 249 ft above sea level and half a mile from the town centre the station boasted one platform 350 ft in length on the up side of the line and long enough to accommodate a six-coach train of bogie corridor stock, and a short bay platform invariably used to stable empty coaching stock. The station platform was originally 300 ft in length and constructed of ballast and shingle between wooden retaining walls but was subsequently rebuilt and lengthened in 1930 with concrete retaining walls and tarmacadam surfacing over part of its length. The signal box at the north end of the platform controlled the points and signals for the run-round loop, bay platform line and access points to the goods yard. The station's accommodation was completed by the usual booking office and waiting rooms on the main platform. The building was extended soon after the opening of the line and then after World War II the SR made considerable alteration by lengthening the building and providing an entirely new roof, which could have been classified as a rebuilding. By the buffer stops in the bay platform stood the cattle loading dock. From 1930 the single line Tablet machine was located in the booking office. The goods yard consisted of three sidings with access obtained by points off the run-round loop, whilst the goods transit shed was situated between the two western sidings together with a small fixed crane of 1 ton 5 cwt capacity later reduced to 15 cwt capacity. To the north of the goods yard was the engine shed, large enough to accommodate the branch tank

The three-arch steel girder bridge with concrete abutments spanning Whalley or Walley Lane, No. 20 at 6 miles 14 chains from Axminster. *Author's Collection*

View from the platform at Lyme Regis looking towards the station throat with milk churns prominent in the foreground. Such traffic was regularly handled until the introduction of diesel-multiple-units on the branch. *Author's Collection*

Double-headed train with '415' class 4-4-2T No. 30583 at the head waiting to depart from Lyme Regis in July 1960; the formation included through coaches to Waterloo. *Author's Collection*

The long shadows cast by the evening sun highlight the Adams radial tank arriving at Lyme Regis in the 1950s with her single-coach train watched by three youngsters, who might be waiting for a passenger to alight. Note the dormitory coach to the far right beyond the goods shed. *Oakwood Collection*

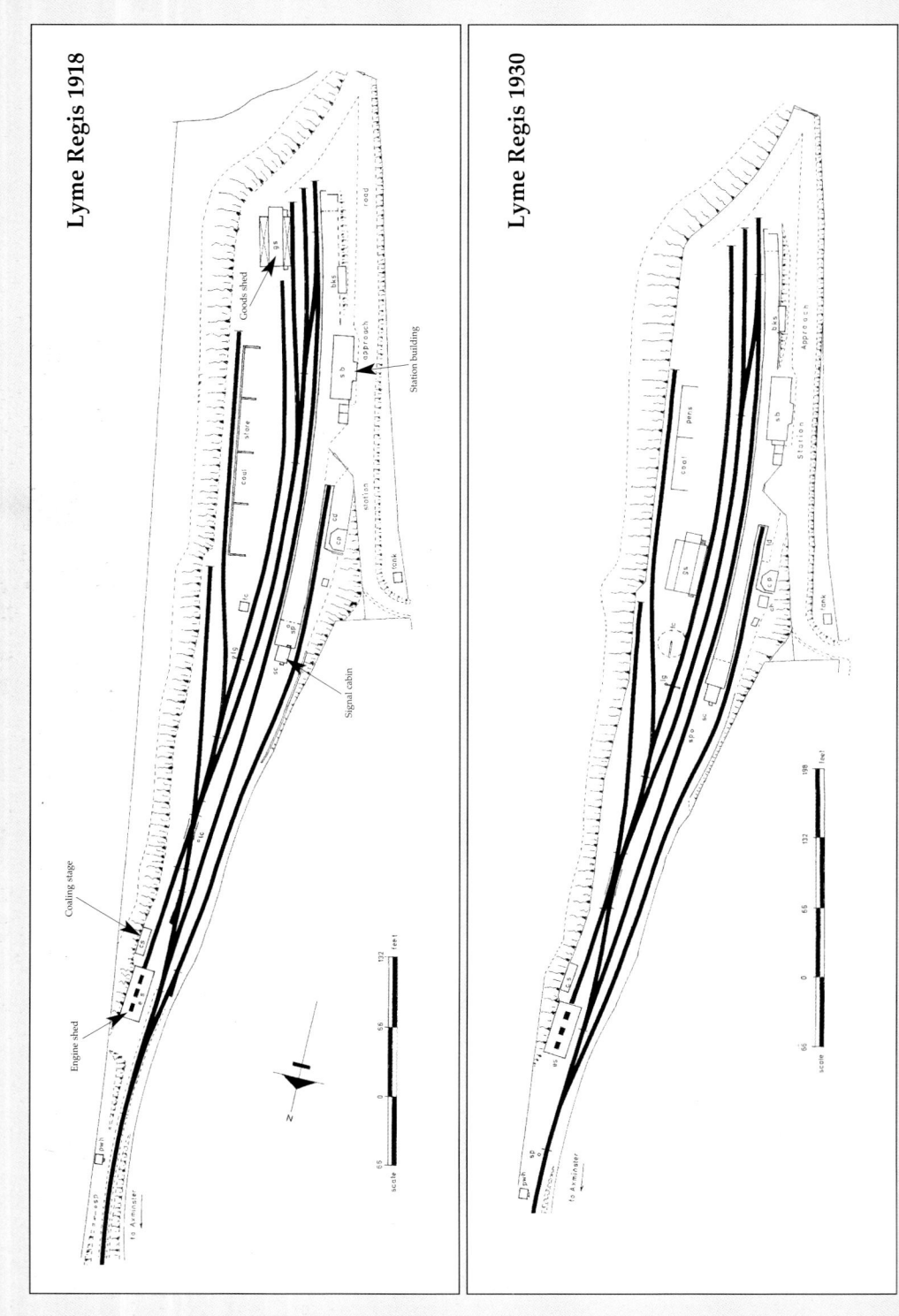

The 1930 alterations at Lyme Regis included the reconstruction of the platform with concrete fascias and metalled surface giving a greater height above rail level. This view looking towards the buffer stops shows the close proximity of the Victoria Hotel to the station. The coach on the right is stabled in the bay platform and will form a through service to Waterloo on the next summer Saturday. *Author's Collection*

General view of Lyme Regis station on the last day of operation; the platform crowded with enthusiasts and local people seeking a last ride on the branch. The former signal box, now bereft of levers, still proudly displays the Lyme Regis sign. *Brian Jackson*

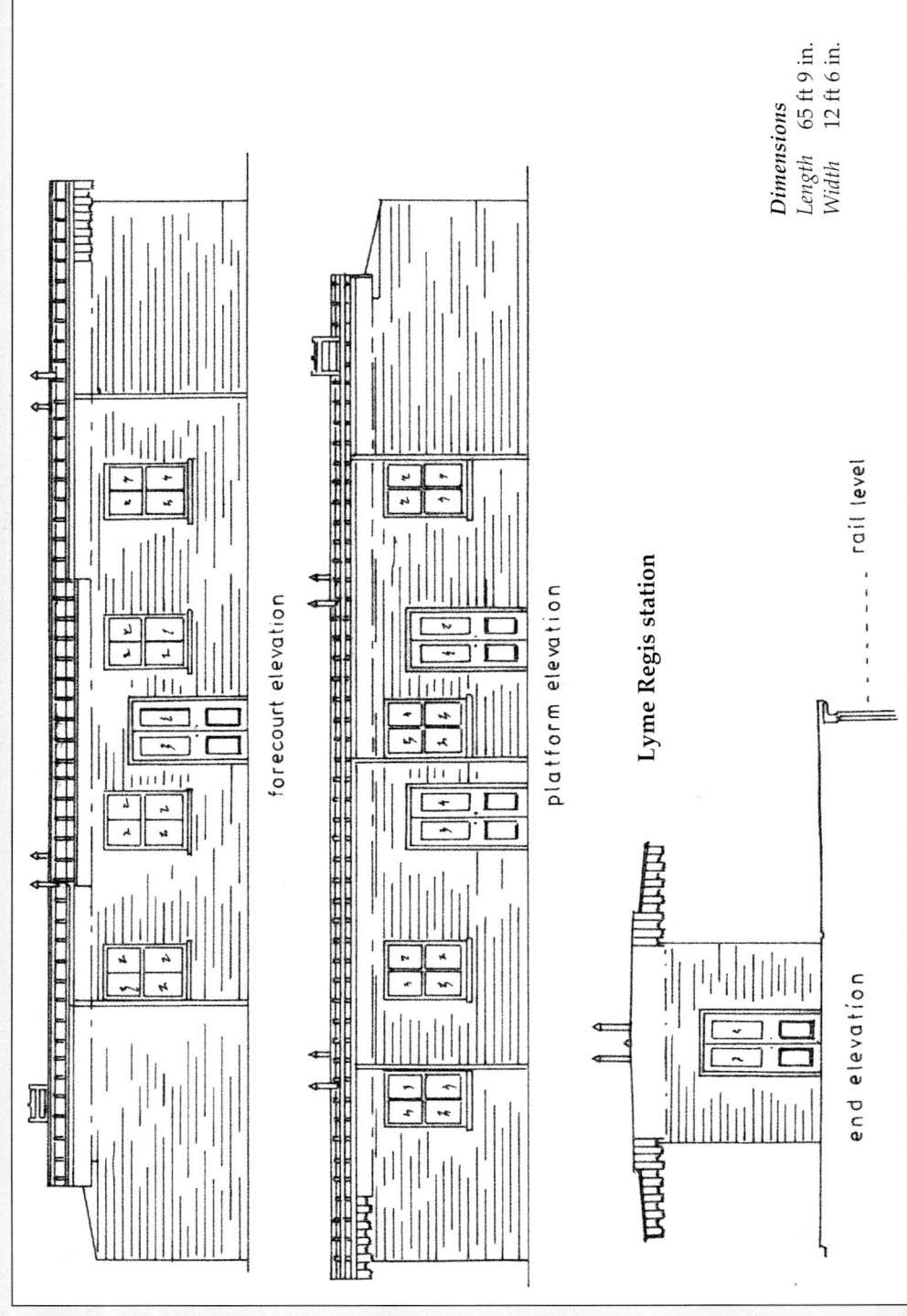

The south end of Lyme Regis station building in original condition soon after the opening of the line. An LSWR 4-wheel brake third can be seen at the platform. *Author's Collection*

External view of Lyme Regis station from the approach road in 1961 with a LMR Ivatt '2MT' class 2-6-2T at the platform. *Author's Collection*

Lyme Regis goods shed

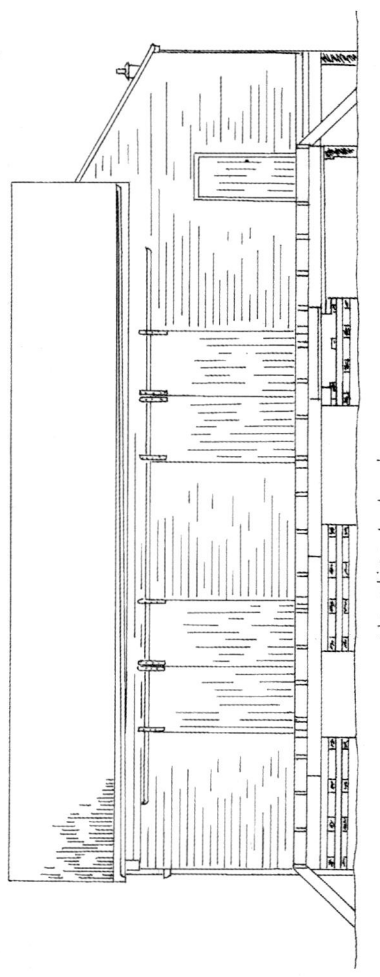

elevation to track

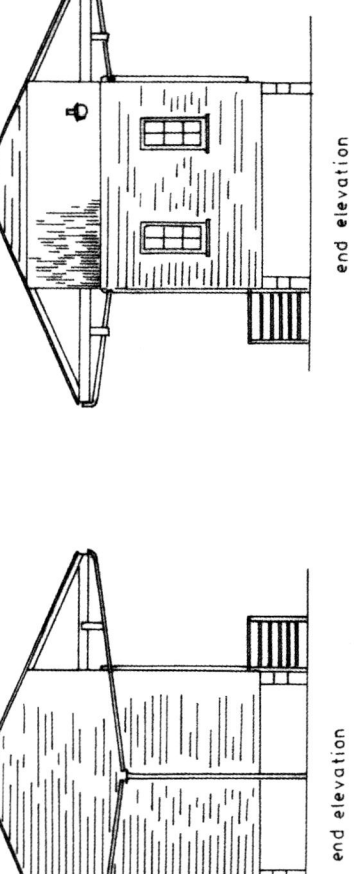

end elevation

end elevation

Dimensions
Length 55 ft 6 in.
Width   15 ft 6 in.

The all-timber goods shed at Lyme Regis viewed from the station platform in 1960 when a small amount of freight traffic was still handled. *Author's Collection*

The south end of Lyme Regis goods shed with the office in the foreground. After the dormitory coach was withdrawn in 1958, Exmouth Junction crews requiring lodging at Lyme Regis occupied one corner of the office. *A.E. West*

The cattle pen and loading dock with concrete facing at Lyme Regis. Little cattle traffic was conveyed on the branch after World War II. *A.E. West*

The 15 cwt capacity (originally 1 ton 5 cwt capacity) fixed crane in the goods yard at Lyme Regis with the signal box in the background. *A.E. West*

The road approach to Lyme Regis station on 7th July, 1959. The access to the goods yard is to the right with a coach stabled against the buffer stops in the run-round loop headshunt.

H.C. Casserley

'415' class 4-4-2T No. 30583 stands by the buffer stops at Lyme Regis prior to running round her train formed of two-coach set No. 44 consisting of brake third No. 2638 (ex-485) to diagram 99 and composite brake 6403 (ex-4652) to diagram 418. These ex-LSWR vehicles were rebuilt and lengthened and placed on new underframes in April 1936 and seated 80 thirds and 10 firsts/38 thirds respectively.

Author's Collection

locomotive, and the adjacent coaling stage and water crane for locomotive replenishment. After closure of the line the station building was resurrected and removed to Alresford on the Mid Hants Railway. Care had to be exercised when shunting the goods yard at Lyme Regis because of the falling gradient to the buffer stops and, although fly shunting was officially banned it was regularly carried out to save time. On occasions a wagon or van had thumped into the buffers fortunately without derailing or damage to the load.

From the station there was a gradual descent by road, which became very steep in the town centre. Good views were obtained from the platform stretching from Chesil Beach in the east to Golden Cap, 619 feet, the highest cliff on the south coast and to Black Ven, another noted landmark. The correspondent for *The Railway Magazine* in 1903 found, 'the scenery of the place undeniably attractive; indeed it would be difficult to find anywhere on the South Coast a finer range of beautiful scenery than that of which Lyme is the centre. Jane Austen compared it to the Isle of Wight, and there is undoubtedly much in common between Lyme and Ventnor, as regards both scenery and climate. As a winter residence for individuals, Lyme Regis should rapidly grow in favour now that the drawback of a six-mile drive from the railway has been removed'.

The distance from the town and inconvenient siting of the station also brought other comments in 1903:

> No attempt is made to get down to the sea level, which as anyone acquainted with Lyme Regis knows, would have been an impossible feat for a railway worked in the ordinary way by ordinary locomotives. In explanation of our use of the word impossible, let us explain that the principal street in Lyme Regis rises very abruptly from the sea, and near the summit of this, at a distance of about half-a-mile from the centre of the place and a height of 250 feet from the shore, the railway terminus has been erected.

The LSWR rather untruthfully announced in their publicity that the walk from station to sea front was only 10 minutes!

Because of its standing as a light railway the speed limit on the branch was restricted to 25 mph, with 10 mph imposed on curves of 9 chains or less. Tender locomotives were also restricted to 15 mph when working tender first, although there is no evidence that tender locomotives ever worked on the branch. Speed over Cannington viaduct was also restricted to 15 mph in the early years of the line, but this was later raised to 25 mph.

Lyme Regis goods yard viewed from the station platform with the goods shed to the left and the coal storage zones, each divided by sleeper partitioning. *A.E. West*

Chapter Six

Permanent Way, Signalling and Staff

Permanent Way

The initial permanent way was formed of flat bottom rail weighing 56 lb. per yard laid in 30 feet lengths and secured to the sleepers by fang bolts and dog spikes. The sleepers measured 9 ft by 9 in. by 4½ inches and the rails were joined by fishplates weighing 13 lb. per pair and secured to the rail by four bolts. The bottom ballast was formed of broken stone laid to a depth of 9 inches below the sleepers and the top ballast was formed of gravel. The original flat bottom track, spiked direct to the sleepers, was soon found inadequate as the 'Terrier's' 12 ft wheelbase spread the track on the curves. Within a fortnight of the opening to traffic the situation had deteriorated to the extent that permanent way staff had to check and adjust the rails and re-ballast in several places. This remedial work sufficed until 1910 when the branch was completely relaid with bullhead rails weighing 75 and 80 lb. per yard, after the 'O2' class 0-4-4Ts had been tried and had inflicted further damage to the formation. Later the line was relaid with second-hand material on LSWR and then SR chairs, the rails initially weighing 75 lb. per yard and later 90 lb. per yard. In 1960 the track was again extensively re-laid, using 95 lb. per yard rail and the curves eased and recanted to allow the introduction of the LMR '2MT' 2-6-2Ts.

Originally ballast was obtained from a site near Combpyne, where a field was purchased for provision of supplies. This was quickly exhausted and supplies then came from other sources, latterly from Meldon Quarry, near Okehampton. When it was necessary to work a loaded ballast train across the branch arrangements were made to have the vehicles hauled by two '415' class 4-4-2T locomotives. Similarly if the weight of empty vehicles presented a hazard on the falling gradients two locomotives were provided for adequate braking.

The permanent way maintenance on the branch was carried out by two gangs, the first working from Axminster to Combpyne and the second from Combpyne to Lyme Regis, although in later years rationalization took place.

Signalling

From the opening of the railway, the branch was worked on the 'One Engine in Steam' with the Train Staff principle. As there were no fixed signals or block telegraph, the train movements were controlled by telephone. Points and signals at Axminster were worked from the signal box except for the points leading from the main single line to the goods yard, which were released by a key attached to the single line Train Staff. The points leading to the siding at Combpyne were operated from a 4-lever ground frame released by the key on the single line Train Staff; similar arrangements were made at Lyme Regis where the 5-lever frame was released by the key attached to the single line Train Staff. Until the LSWR took over the operation of the line a flagman was positioned at the end of Cannington viaduct to signal trains across and keep watch for subsidence or movements in the structure.

From 19th September, 1906 the electric tablet was introduced for single line working using Tyer's No. 6 Tablet instruments with Sykes interlocking. The line was

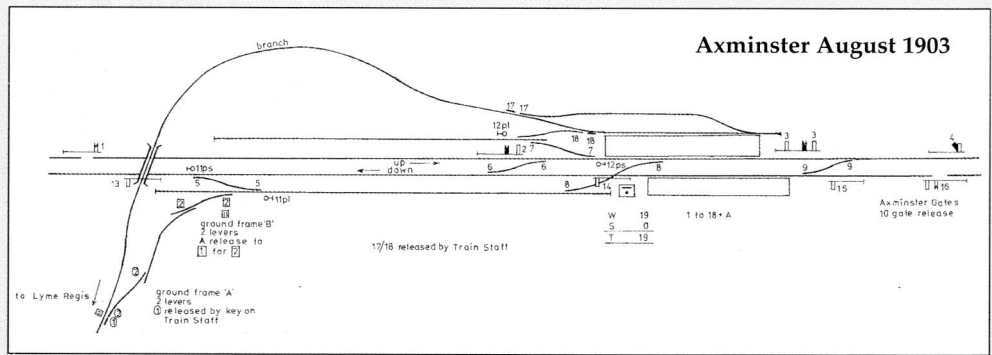

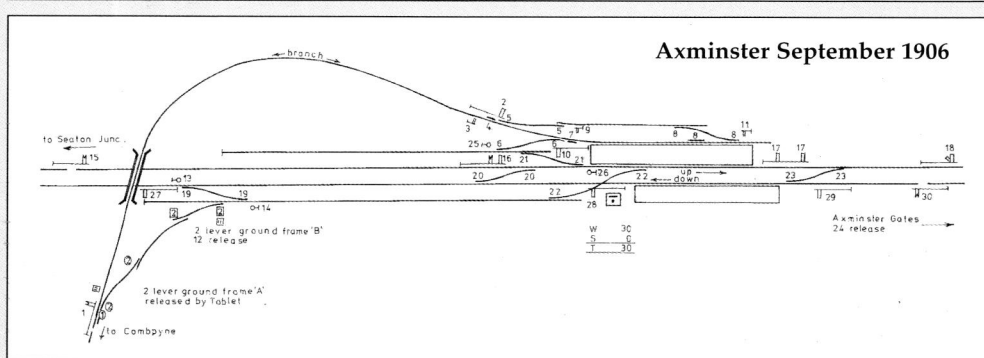

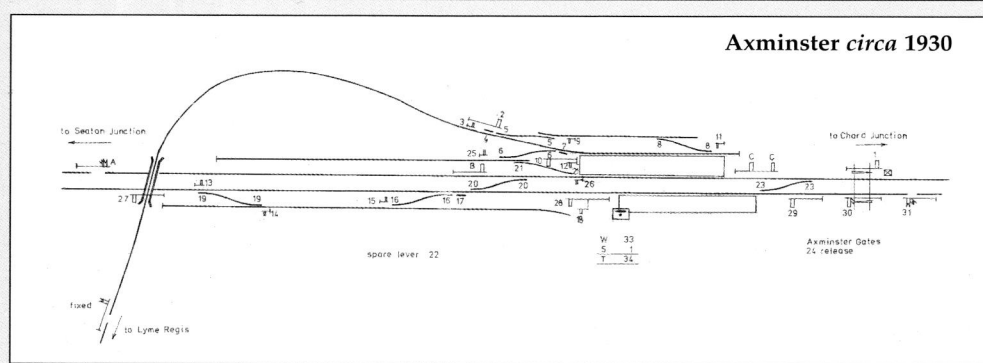

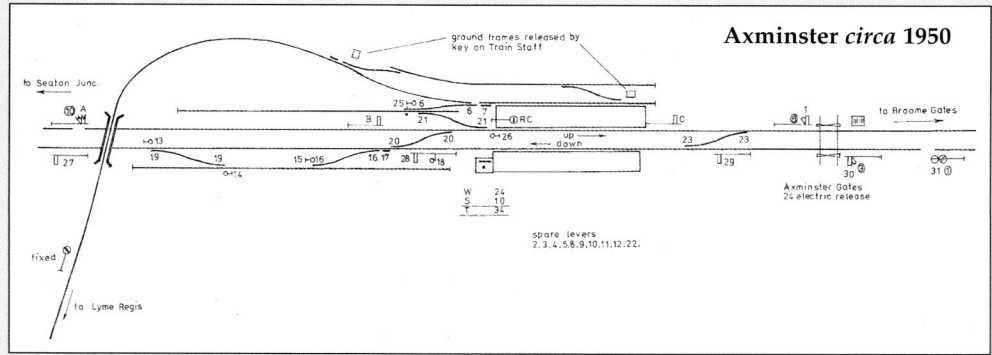

PERMANENT WAY, SIGNALLING AND STAFF

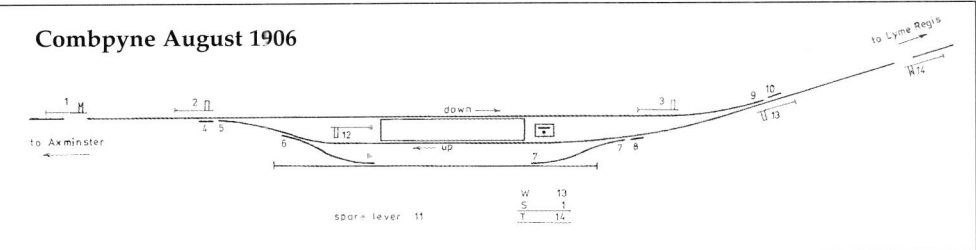

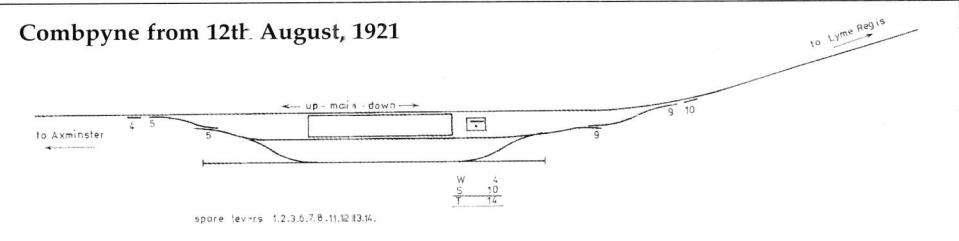

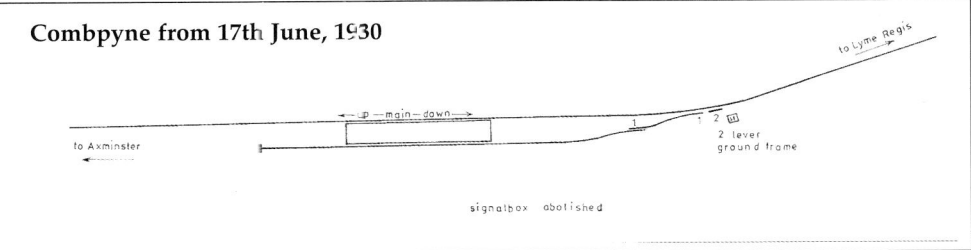

The former Combpyne signal box of similar design to that at Lyme Regis in remarkably good condition in 1961 after serving as shed, hen house and other purposes on a local farm for over 30 years. *Author's Collection*

Looking north from the platform at Lyme Regis towards the station throat in 1960.
Author's Collection

'415' class No. 3125 running past Lyme Regis signal box and into the station platform with a down train. The locomotive carries the correct route headcode of one disc on the centre of the bufferbeam, the disc also displaying the Lyme Regis shed duty code No. 502. The up starting signal beyond the signal box now has an upper quadrant arm. *A.E. West*

divided into two sections Axminster to Combpyne and Combpyne to Lyme Regis, with ground level signal boxes at both Combpyne and Lyme Regis and fixed signals installed at Axminster, Combpyne and Lyme Regis. From 27th March, 1960 the line reverted to 'One Engine in Steam' operation using the single line Train Staff. At Axminster it was usual for a designated porter to collect the Train Staff or Tablet from the driver of the branch train but at busy periods any person delegated by the station master including the signalman would perform the task.

At Axminster all points and signals came under the control of the main line signal box dating from 1875 initially equipped with a 16-lever Stevens Tappet frame with 4⅛ in. centres. From 19th August, 1903 this was extended to 19 levers and from July 1906 to incorporate the workings of the new light railway was again extended to 30 levers and finally from 1938 to 34 levers. The down side connection was operated from two 2-lever ground frames. Except for minor alterations and the removal of the connection on the down side via the goods yard to the branch, the layout remained essentially the same throughout the history of the line. The signal box was abolished as a result of main line rationalization on 5th March, 1967.

Combpyne signal box located at the east end of the platform ramp originally had a 14-lever Stevens design Railway Signal Co. Tappet knee frame with 4⅝ in. centres with 13 working and one spare lever. In the early 1920s economies were sought and from 12th August, 1921 all signal arms were removed leaving only the points to the loop siding operated from the signal box, which now had four working and 10 spare levers; thereafter all passenger trains used the single main line. The Tyer's No. 6 Tablet instrument was also removed and the branch became one single line section, Axminster to Lyme Regis, with the tablet suitably inscribed. The layout at Combpyne was again altered on and from 17th June, 1930, when the signal box, signals, up loop line and facing points at the Axminster end of the station were abolished. The former up loop line was shortened and straightened at the west end to become a siding with access gained by facing points in the up direction at the Lyme Regis end of the station, controlled from a 2-lever ground frame, locked and unlocked by a key or the Tablet.

Lyme Regis signal box, alike in appearance and size to Combpyne also boasted a 14-lever Stevens design Dutton knee frame with all levers working and later with 13 working and one spare lever. As the years progressed the 14-lever frame had eventually 11 working and three spares and later nine working levers and five spares. The distance from Axminster signal box located at the west end of the down main line platform to Lyme Regis signal box was 6 miles 1,098 yards. Lyme Regis signal box was abolished on 20th July, 1965.

For the branch Axminster signal box controlled a down starter and up distant which was fixed and an up home signal. At Combpyne prior to rationalization in 1921 the signal box controlled distant, home and starting signals for each direction of travel but these were removed as the result of rationalization on and from 12th August, 1921. At Lyme Regis a down fixed distant guarded the down home signal; in the up direction starting and advance starting signals were provided. From the early 1950s, SR upper quadrant signal arms replaced the original LSWR lower quadrant semaphore signal arms.

At the same time as the rationalization at Combpyne (1930), the Tablet instrument at Lyme Regis was removed from the signal box and placed in the parcels office so that the porter/signalman could be employed on station duties when not required for signalling train movements. This arrangement was retained until after the cessation of goods working and from 27th March, 1960 the signal box was reduced in status to a ground frame when the points were clipped and the line reverted to 'One Engine in Steam' working until complete closure.

end elevation

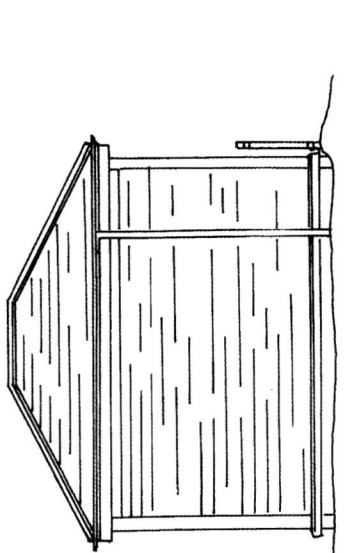

end elevation

Lyme Regis signal box

Dimensions
Length 16 ft 6 in.
Width   11 ft 6 in.

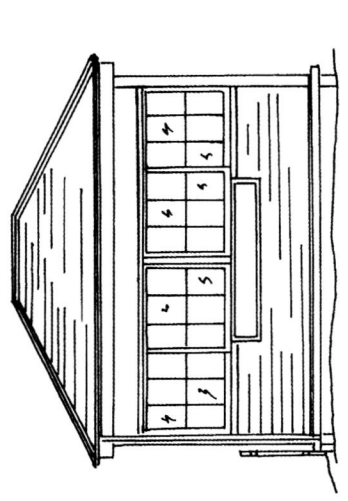

front elevation

rear elevation

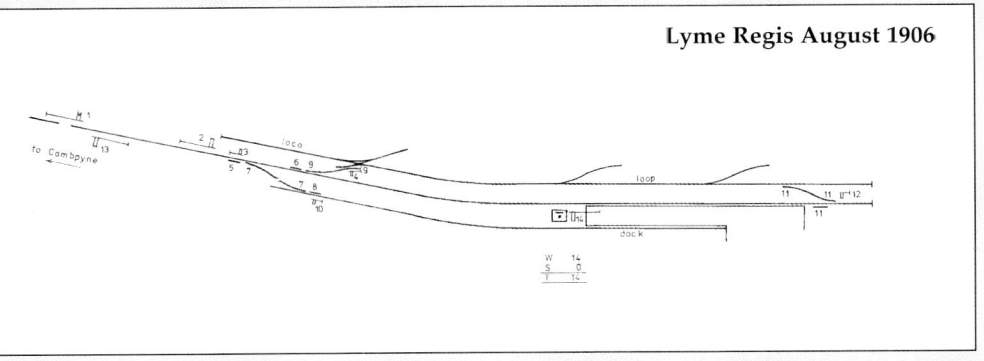

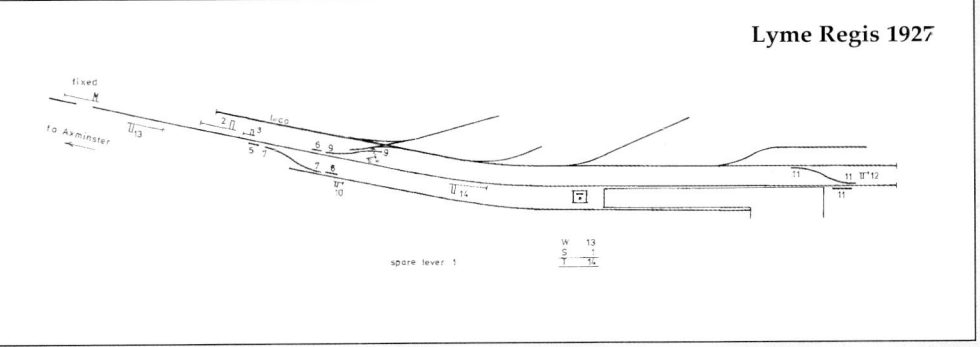

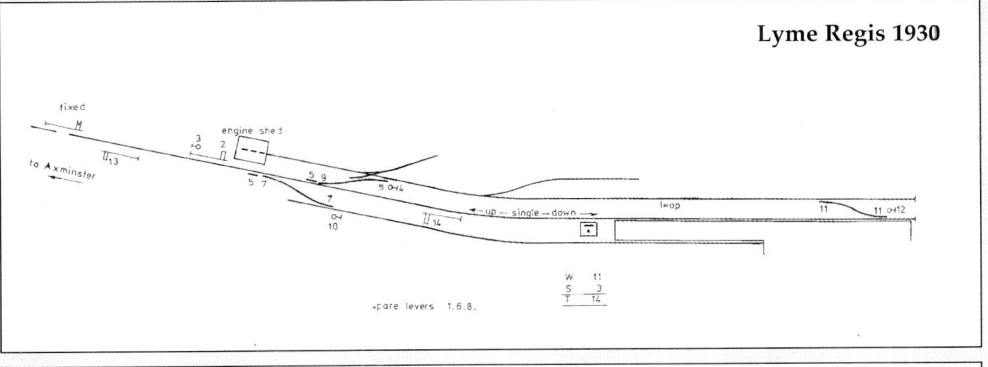

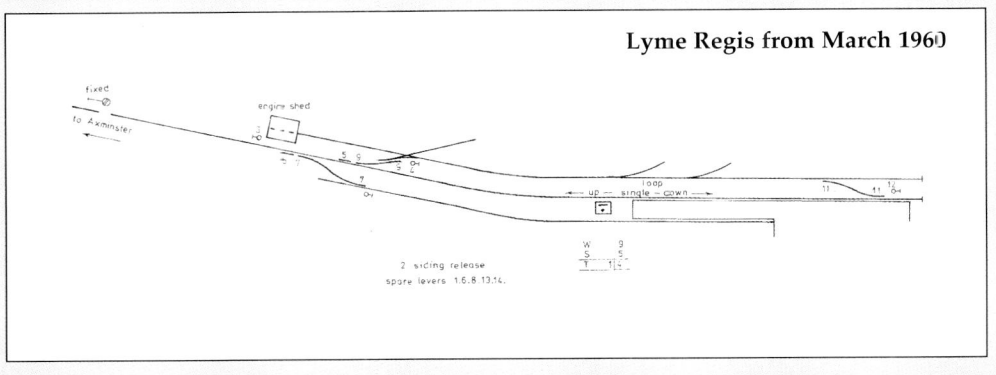

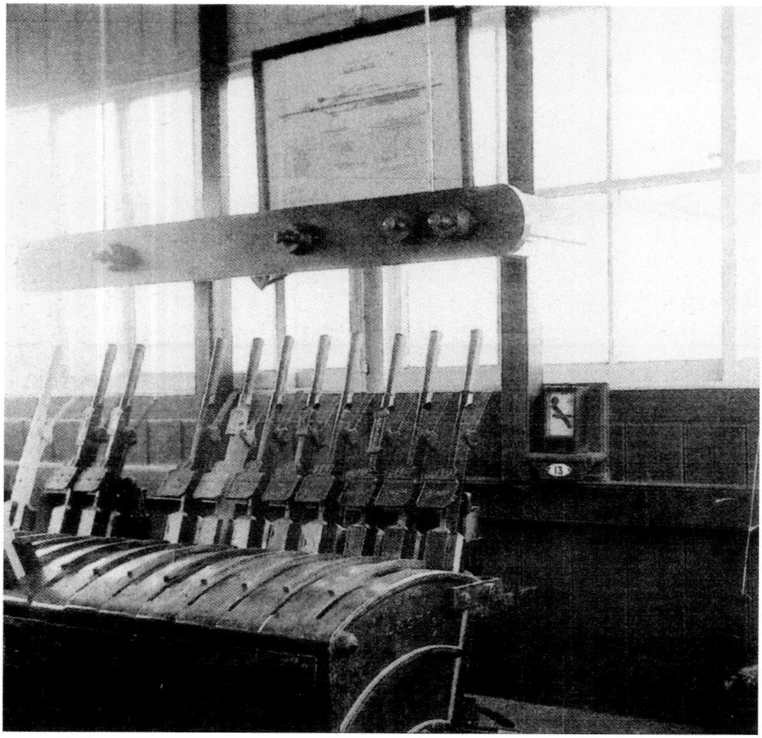

PERMANENT WAY, SIGNALLING AND STAFF

Above: Lyme Regis signal box containing a 14-lever frame was provided in 1906 with the introduction of Electric Tablet working of the single line. The tablet instrument was subsequently removed and placed in the station booking office enabling the porter/signalman to expand his duties from signalling trains to also issuing tickets. The wooden nameboard, with cast letters, was later replaced by a BR green enamel sign mounted on the Axminster end of the signal box. *A. Cullen*

Top left: The 14-lever Stevens' design Dutton knee-frame with 13 working and one spare lever in Lyme Regis signal box. The indicator for the up advanced starting signal (lever No. 13) is behind the frame, as the signal could not be seen from the signal box. *A.E. West*

Bottom left: The south aspect of Lyme Regis signal box, displaying an array of fire buckets, with the up starting signal in the background. This signal was repositioned when the platform was extended to accommodate longer trains, having previously been in front of the box.
A.E. West

The footplate crew of class '415' class No. 3520 take a moment's relaxation as they await departure from Lyme Regis. On the left can be seen the private owner wagon of local coal merchant W.H. Thomas & Son, who traded at both Axminster and Lyme Regis.

Author's Collection

Driver and guard pass conversation as the former heads for the cab of No. 30582 at Axminster. Note the locomotive has bespoke wooden shuttering in the cab to protect enginemen from the icy winds of autumn and winter.

Author's Collection

Staff

The branch was quite generously staffed in the early years when even Combpyne boasted station master and porter/signalman until 1930 when the crossing loop was removed; as a result of the rationalization the station master's post was abolished and a leading porter appointed. For many years the incumbent covered permanent early turn whilst relief staff covered the back shift and holiday and sickness cover. At Lyme Regis the establishment, subject to minor variations over the years, consisted of station master, two booking clerks, two porter/signalmen, two porters and goods porter and two guards. The station master also had charge of the two drivers, two firemen and engine cleaner for administration purposes.

Station masters

When the line opened in 1903 Charles Henry Ley formerly employed at Poole was appointed as station master at Lyme Regis to be followed by E.R. Martin. From 1916 until 1947 Arthur Clement Stretch was in charge before being succeeded by W.J. Rooks. Four years later Rooks was promoted to Christchurch and William H. Mairs, promoted from Mortehoe, assumed responsibility for the branch. The last incumbent before closure was A.H. Causley. Combpyne had a station master from 1903 until 1930, the first and only holder being R. Greenslade. During the life of the branch from 1903 station masters at Axminster were Messrs Budd and Hayter, then W.J. Grayer from 1938 to 1955 followed by Messrs Wood, Shepherd and Phare until the post was withdrawn in 1964.

Traffic staff

Of note H. Blanchard, porter/signalman at Lyme Regis, later became mayor of the town and it was he who performed the naming ceremony of Bulleid Pacific No. 21C109 *Lyme Regis* at Axminster station in 1946. Brothers Len and Ken Enticott served at Combpyne but in the latter years Mike Clements who commenced his railway career in 1961 and Nolly Forster shared duties as porters at the intermediate station. Guard Thomas Edworthy served on the branch, whilst Donald King was porter/signalman at Lyme Regis in the last years.

1st JUNE to 30th SEPTEMBER, 1909, or until further notice.

LYME REGIS LIGHT RAILWAY.

FOR SPEED RESTRICTIONS SEE PAGES A, B, C & D.

This is a Single Line and is worked under the Regulations for working Single Lines by the Electric Train Tablet Block System.

WEEK DAYS—NO SUNDAY SERVICE.

Distance from Axminster	DOWN TRAINS.	1 Pass.		2		3 Mixed.		4 Goods.		5		6 Mixed.		7		8 Mixed. June 1st to July 9th inc. and from Sept. 27th.		9 Mixed. July 10th to Sept. 25th inclusive.		10
M. C.		arr. a.m.	dep. a.m.			arr. a.m.	dep. a.m.	arr. a.m.	dep. a.m.			arr. p.m.	dep. p.m.			arr. p.m.	dep. p.m.	arr. p.m.	dep. p.m.	
— —	AXMINSTER	...	8 5	...	...	...	10 37	...	11 50	...	...	...	1 10	...	...	...	3 0	...	3 10	
4 21	Combpyne	8 17	8 18	...	...	After No. 1 Up arrives. 10 49	10 50	After No. 5 Up arrives. 12 10	12 13	...	...	After No. 6 Up arrives. 1 22	1 23	...	...	After No. 8 Up arrives. 3 12	3 13	After No. 8 Up arrives. 3 22	3 23	
6 59	LYME REGIS	8 25	...	...	...	10 57	...	12 20	...	...	...	1 30	...	...	...	3 20	...	3 30	...	

	DOWN TRAINS.	11 Pass.		12 Mixed.		13 Mixed.		14 Mixed.		15		16		17		18		19		20
		arr. p.m.	dep. p.m.	arr. p.m.	dep. p.m.	arr. p.m.	dep. p.m.	arr. p.m.	dep. p.m.											
	AXMINSTER	...	4 27	...	5 50	...	7 12	...	8 45	...	...	...	...	...	...	...	...	...	...	
	Combpyne	After No. 12 Up arrives. 4 39	4 40	After No. 13 Up arrives. 6 2	6 3	After No. 14 Up arrives. 7 24	7 25	After No. 15 Up arrives. 8 57	8 58	...	...	...	...	...	...	...	...	...	...	
	LYME REGIS	4 47	...	6 10	...	7 32	...	9 5	...	...	...	...	...	...	...	...	...	...	...	

Distance from Lyme Regis	UP TRAINS.	1 Pass.		2 Pass. Fridays only.		3 Pass. Not Fridays.		4 Goods.		5 Mixed.		6		7		8 Mixed. A		9		10
M. C.		arr. a.m.	dep. a.m.	arr. a.m.	dep. a.m.	arr. a.m.	dep. a.m.	arr. a.m.	dep. a.m.	arr. p.m.	dep. p.m.					arr. p.m.	dep. p.m.			
— —	LYME REGIS	...	7 12	...	9 38	...	9 47	...	11 12	...	12 30	...	...	...	...	...	2 20	...	...	
2 38	Combpyne	7 20	7 21	After No. 1 Dn. arrives. 9 46	9 47	After No. 1 Down arrives. 9 56	9 57	After No. 3 Down arrives. 11 21	11 24	After No. 4 Dn. arrives. 12 38	12 39	...	...	...	...	After No. 6 Down arrives. 2 28	2 29	...	...	
6 59	AXMINSTER	7 32	...	...	...	9 58	...	10 8	...	11 36	...	12 50	...	...	...	2 40	...	...	...	

	UP TRAINS.	11		12 Pass.		13 Mixed.		14 Mixed.		15 Mixed.		16		17		18		19		20
				arr. p.m.	dep. p.m.	arr. p.m.	dep. p.m.	arr. p.m.	dep. p.m.	arr. p.m.	dep. p.m.									
	LYME REGIS	...	...	...	3 55	...	4 55	...	6 30	...	8 15	...	...	...	...	...	...	...	...	
	Combpyne	...	...	After Nos. 8 or 9 Dwn. arrs. 4 3	4 4	After No. 11 Down arrives. 5 3	5 4	After No. 12 Down arrives. 6 38	6 39	After No. 13 Down arrives. 8 23	8 24	...	...	...	...	...	...	...	...	
	AXMINSTER	...	...	...	4 15	...	5 15	...	6 50	...	8 35	...	...	...	...	...	...	...	...	

A Vac. Road Box Lyme Regis to Nine Elms by this Train.

The load of Passenger and Mixed Trains must not exceed 40 wheels. The load of Down Goods Trains may be made up to 48 wheels when not more than 6 loads of coal or equally heavy minerals. The load of Up Goods Trains may be 60 wheels when it consists principally of empty wagons.

LSWR working timetable 1909.

Chapter Seven

Timetables and Traffic

After taking almost six decades to bring a railway to Lyme Regis the Directors of the light railway company hoped their efforts would result in a large expansion of business, an increase in the population and, last but not least, a revival of the holiday trade, which had been in decline. Initially the signs were encouraging as freight transferred from a seaborne source to the new railway, whilst there was a slight increase in the population, which ultimately tailed off until after World War II, as the figure below show. Certainly holiday traffic was encouraged with through coaches to and from London Waterloo except during the two periods of hostility. However, the season was short and for many months of each year passenger traffic was sparse, being handled in one-coach trains, and freight almost non-existent. Nevertheless the branch served the locality with quiet efficiency for the six decades of its existence in the evolution of transport on the Devon/Dorset border.

Year	1901	1911	1921	1931	1951	1961
Axminster	2,933	2,854	2,662	3,320	4,063	4,285
Combpyne	146	146	140	137	127	89
Uplyme	798	833	568	1,005	1,165	1,243
Lyme Regis	2,095	2,772	2,882	2,620	3,200	3,526
Total branch only	*3,039*	*3,751*	*3,590*	*3,762*	*4,492*	*4,858*
Total including Axminster	*5,972*	*6,605*	*6,252*	*7,082*	*8,555*	*9,143*

The initial train service from 24th August, 1903 consisted of six trains in each direction on weekdays only with departures from Lyme Regis at 9.40 am, 12.25, 2.10, 4.50, 6.10 and 8.05 pm returning from Axminster at 10.45 am, 1.18, 2.56, 5.32, 6.50 and 8.50 pm. Trains were allowed 25 minutes for the journey and departures from Combpyne were 13 and 18 minutes later than Lyme Regis and Axminster respectively. The fastest journey time from Waterloo to Lyme Regis was achieved in 4 hours 10 minutes. The *Bridport News* reported the times had been 'arranged with a view to meeting the convenience of, not only townspeople, but of passengers on the main line'. However, complaints were soon voiced regarding the early evening departure of the last up train at 8.05 pm, especially during the summer months when a later departure from Lyme Regis would have benefited day-trippers from Axminster and Chard. The LSWR authorities at Waterloo rejected a petition for the late train to depart Lyme Regis at 9.15 pm.

By 1907 the journey time on the branch was reduced by 5 minutes with passenger trains departing Lyme Regis at 7.20, 9.40 am Fridays only (FO), 9.50 am Fridays excepted (FX), 12.30 mixed, 2.18 mixed, 3.55, 4.55 mixed, 6.15 mixed and 8.15 pm mixed. The return trains from Axminster departed at 8.05, 10.37 am mixed, 1.15 mixed, 2.55 mixed, 4.27, 5.50 mixed, 6.47 mixed and 8.45 pm mixed. Combpyne departures were 13 minutes later than Axminster on the down road and nine minutes later than Lyme Regis on up journeys. The branch goods train departed Lyme Regis at 11.12 am and was allowed 12 minutes to Combpyne and 12 minutes thence to Axminster arriving at 11.36 am. The goods train returned from Axminster at 11.50 am with 13 minutes allowed to Combpyne and 17 minutes thence to Lyme Regis arriving at 12.20 pm.

From July 1908 the LSWR introduced through coaches from Waterloo to Lyme Regis and return and the facility was retained during each summer timetable. In the same year the massive geological landslip in the cliffs to the south of Combpyne caused the ground to catch fire, the inferno burning for almost eight months bringing an unexpected increase in traffic and passenger services were enhanced to cater for the additional sightseers. In 1909 the weekday service on the branch consisted of eight passenger services and one goods train in each direction, of which five of the former were classified as mixed to convey goods traffic not taken by the freight service. The first up train departed Lyme Regis at 7.12 am and the last down train departed Axminster at 8.45 pm.

By the summer of 1910 the journey time from Waterloo to Lyme Regis had been reduced to 3 hours 30 minutes whilst the time table for 1911 showed departures from Lyme Regis at 7.07, 9.38 FO, 9.48 am FX, 12.30, 2.20, 3.55, 4.55, 6.30 and 8.13 pm with returning services from Axminster at 8.05, 10.37 am, 1.08, 3.00, 4.27, 5.50, 7.15 and 8.45 pm.

The LSWR public timetable for 1914 showed the following service on weekdays only,

			M	M	A	B				
		am	am	am	pm	pm	pm	pm	pm	pm	pm
Axminster	dep.	8.00	10.23	11.57	1.20	3.15	3.23	4.30	5.55	7.17	8.55
Combpyne	dep.	8.13	10.38	12.10	1.35	3.28	3.36	4.43	6.08	7.30	9.08
Lyme Regis	arr.	8.20	10.45	12.17	1.42	3.35	3.43	4.50	6.15	7.37	9.15

					M	M			
		am	am	am	pm	pm	pm	pm	pm	pm
Lyme Regis	dep.	7.27	9.30	11.20	12.30	2.20	3.53	5.00	6.35	8.05
Combpyne	dep.	7.36	9.39	11.29	12.39	2.30	4.07	5.09	6.44	8.14
Axminster	arr.	7.47	9.50	11.40	12.50	2.41	4.18	5.20	6.55	8.25

A – 17th July-19th September excepted, B – 17th July-19th September inclusive
M – mixed train

Although traffic declined during World War I services were not greatly affected save that the through coaches to and from Waterloo had been withdrawn after the 1914 summer service. The timetable thereafter settled down to a routine, which was to last until the advent of the Southern Railway. The final pre-Grouping timetable showing nine passenger trains in each direction weekdays-only commencing with the 8.15 am ex-Lyme Regis and finishing with the 9.12 pm ex-Axminster, each allowed 20 minutes running time. One goods train ran in each direction but no Sunday services were offered. By the summer of 1925 the weekdays-only service still retained similarity to that of the LSWR regime with departures from Lyme Regis at 8.15, 9.30, 10.23 FO, 11.23 am, 1.03, 2.03, 4.00, 5.15 and 8.20 pm returning from Axminster at 8.55, 9.55 FO, 10.25 FX, 10.55 am FO, 12.39, 1.39, 3.12, 4.44, 6.22, 7.50 and 8.52 pm.

The timetable from 25th March, 1928 showed the following weekdays-only service of eight passenger trains in each direction:

Down		am	am	pm	pm	pm	pm	pm	pm
Axminster	dep.	8.45	10.25	12.25	2.15	3.25	4.38	6.42	8.52
Combpyne	dep.	8.58	10.38	12.38	2.28	3.38	4.51	6.55	9.05
Lyme Regis	arr.	9.05	10.45	12.45	2.35	3.45	4.58	7.02	9.12

TIMETABLES AND TRAFFIC 99

Up		am	am	am	pm	pm	pm	pm	pm
Lyme Regis	dep.	8.15	9.30	11.40	1.45	2.45	3.55	5.08	8.20
Combpyne	dep.	8.24	9.39	11.49	1.54	2.54	4.04	5.17	8.29
Axminster	arr.	8.35	9.50	12.00	2.05	3.05	4.15	5.28	8.40

After local petitioning, summer Sunday services were introduced from 30th June, 1930 when seven down and six up trains were operated for the duration of the season until withdrawn on 21st September. This timetable also saw the through coaches restored on summer Saturdays between Waterloo and Lyme Regis and the arrangement continued during each summer season until the outbreak of World War II.

The timetable for 1932 showed the following service:

Weekdays

											sn SO
Down		am	am	am	pm	pm	pm	pm	pm	pm	pm
Axminster	dep.	8.35	9.40	10.43	12.25	2.40	4.12	5.40	6.38	8.50	9.40
Combpyne	dep.	8.47	9.52	10.55	12.37	2.52	4.24	5.52	6.50	9.02	–
Lyme Regis	arr.	8.55	10.00	11.03	12.45	3.00	4.32	6.00	6.58	9.10	10.02

Sundays until 25th September

		am	am	pm	pm	pm	pm	pm	pm	pm	pm	pm
Axminster	dep.	10.22	11.17	12.16	1.18	2.40	4.02	5.30	6.30	7.38	8.50	10.30
Combpyne	dep.	10.34	11.29	12.28	1.30	2.52	4.14	5.42	6.42	7.50	9.02	10.42
Lyme Regis	arr.	10.42	11.37	12.36	1.38	3.00	4.23	5.50	6.50	7.58	9.10	10.50

Sundays from 2nd October

		sn pm	sn pm	sn pm	sn pm
Axminster	dep.	2.45	4.30	5.50	6.25
Combpyne	dep.	–	–	–	–
Lyme Regis	arr.	3.09	4.54	6.14	7.04

Weekdays

		sn									sn SO
Up		am	am	am	am	am	pm	pm	pm	pm	pm	pm
Lyme Regis	dep.	7.22	8.05	9.10	10.05	11.50	1.55	3.40	4.42	6.10	8.20	9.15
Combpyne	dep.	–	8.13	9.18	10.13	11.58	2.03	3.48	4.50	6.18	8.28	–
Axminster	arr.	7.49	8.25	9.30	10.25	12.10	2.15	4.00	5.02	6.30	8.40	9.42

Sundays until 25th September

		am	am	am	pm	pm	pm	pm	pm	pm	pm	pm
Lyme Regis	dep.	9.55	10.50	11.49	12.45	1.48	3.30	5.00	5.56	7.10	8.15	9.45
Combpyne	dep.	10.03	10.58	11.57	12.53	1.56	3.38	5.08	6.04	7.18	8.23	9.53
Axminster	arr.	10.15	11.10	12.09	1.05	2.08	3.50	5.20	6.16	7.30	8.35	10.05

Sundays from 2nd October

		sn pm	sn pm	sn pm	sn pm	sn pm
Lyme Regis	dep.	1.53	2.53	3.53	4.53	5.43
Combpyne	dep.	–	–	–	–	–
Axminster	arr.	2.20	3.20	4.20	5.20	6.10

sn – Southern National bus, not serving Combpyne. SO – Saturdays only.

'415' class No. 3125 in plain black SR livery prepares to run-round her train at Axminster in August 1948. To the left are the down and up main lines whilst the branch can be seen curving away to the right before swinging left over the main lines. After running round the engine will propel the coaches back down the platform to ease loading of passengers and parcels. The coaching stock is set 44 consisting of non-gangwayed lavatory brake composite and brake third modified in 1935/36 by placing 48 ft LSWR bodies suitably lengthened on 58 ft SR underframes.
D. Clayton

The 12.33 pm Lyme Regis to Axminster train hauled by '415' class No. 30584 descending the gradient away from Combpyne and over Combpyne Farm bridge, No. 13 at 4 miles 15 chains, on 30th August, 1953.
S.C. Nash

In the late 1930s the branch timings were increased from 20 to 21 minutes and by 1939 the summer Sunday services remained at 11 trains in each direction with the 6.38 pm departure from Lyme Regis running non-stop to Axminster in 19 minutes. A similar timing was achieved with the 10.28 am SO train from Lyme Regis. The 1939 timetable showed weekday departures from Lyme Regis: 7.37 SN bus, 8.04, 9.09, 10.05, 10.28 SO, 11.47 Saturdays excepted (SX), 11.53 am SO, 1.14, 2.12 SO, 2.13 SX, 3.55 SX, 4.00 SO, 5.05 SX, 5.10 SO, 6.04 SX, 6.15 SO, 6.58 Wednesdays and Saturdays only (WSO), 7.28 Wednesdays only (WO) and 8.21 pm Wednesdays excepted (WX), whilst Sunday trains departed at 9.52, 10.50, 11.48 am, 1.08, 2.14, 3.23, 5.30, 6.26, 7.18, 8.15 and 9.36 pm. Weekday departures from Axminster were 8.33 SX, 8.37 SO, 9.39, 10.41 SX, 11.26 am SO, 12.32 WSX, 12.46 WSO, 1.47 SX, 2.46 SX, 3.18 SO, 4.28 SX, 4.35 SO, 5.38 SX, 5.40 SO, 6.03 FX, 6.58 FO, 7.25 WSX, 8.35 SX, 9.00 pm SN bus. Sunday departures were 10.24, 11.16 am, 12.33, 1.47, 2.45, 4.30, 5.59, 6.53, 7.58, 9.08 and 10.40 pm. The 10.28 am SO ex-Lyme Regis and the Sunday 6.53 pm ex-Axminster ran non-stop.

World War II put a halt to the expanding timetable but in October 1940 a winter Sunday service was introduced with seven trains in each direction to cope with the loss of road transport because of fuel rationing. By February 1942 the following weekday service operated in the down direction departing Axminster at 8.35, 10.43 am, 12.45, 1.47, 2.47, 4.33, 5.38, 6.45 and 8.55 pm and in the up direction from Lyme Regis at 8.04, 10.05 am, 12.09, 1.14, 2.13, 3.55, 5.10, 6.04 and 8.21 pm. Trains called at Combpyne 12 minutes after departing Axminster and 8 minutes after leaving Lyme Regis, the overall running time across the branch being 21 minutes. On Sundays the following service operated.

Down		am	pm	pm	pm	pm	pm	pm
Axminster	dep.	11.16	12.40	3.00	4.35	5.50	7.33	8.30
Combpyne	dep.	11.28	12.52	3.12	4.47	6.02	7.45	8.42
Lyme Regis	arr.	11.37	1.01	3.21	4.56	6.11	7.54	8.51
Up		am	am	pm	pm	pm	pm	pm
Lyme Regis	dep.	10.45	11.42	2.25	4.05	5.10	7.00	7.58
Combpyne	dep.	10.53	11.50	2.33	4.13	5.18	7.08	8.05
Axminster	arr.	11.06	12.03	2.46	4.26	5.31	7.21	8.18

After the hostilities the passenger service was increased but not to the proportions of pre-war days and the last summer timetable under SR ownership for 1947 showed weekday departures from Lyme Regis at 7.20 SN bus, 8.04, 10.00, 11.15 SO, 11.34 am SX, 12.09 SO, 12.29 SX, 1.24, 2.19 SX, 2.39 SO, 3.55, 5.10, 6.05 and 8.20 pm whilst Sunday services left at 10.40, 11.37 am, 2.35, 3.50, 5.10, 7.00 and 7.58 pm. Axminster departures on weekdays were 8.35, 10.43, 11.42 am SO, 12.02 SX, 12.45 SO, 12.57 SX, 1.53 SX, 2.00 SO, 2.50 SX, 3.20 SO, 4.40, 5.38, 6.50, 8.55 and 9.45 pm SN bus. Sunday departures were 11.11 am, 12.40, 3.10, 4.20, 5.50, 7.33 and 8.30pm.

A separate freight service continued to run across the branch and in 1949, the up train departed Lyme Regis at 6.15 am with arrival at Axminster at 6.35 am. After shunting the yard the return working departed the junction at 7.23 am and with 10 minutes allowed for shunting at Combpyne arrival at Lyme Regis was at 7.53 am, in time for the locomotive to work the 8.04 am passenger train to Axminster. If urgent goods required transit the 10.43 am ex-Axminster and 4.00 pm ex-Lyme Regis passenger trains were permitted to run as mixed trains.

The collection of through coach or coaches from Waterloo to Lyme Regis at Axminster required a complex operational move to get the vehicle or vehicles on to the branch train for forward transit to the final destination. Here down starting signal No. 28 is clear to allow Radial tank No. 30582, which has just collected the single coach detached from the down main line train, to run forward past the signal box before reversing over crossover No. 20 to the up main line. The engine and coach would then stand in the up main platform before running forward using No. 21 crossover to gain access into the up siding. A further reversing movement over No. 6 crossover allowed the coach or coaches to be attached to the branch train standing in the bay platform. The journey would then continue to Lyme Regis. *Oakwood Collection*

'415' class No. 30584 standing at Lyme Regis with the single coach branch train formed of 'BCK' from set No. 108. The partially canopied platform and station building are to the left, whilst the points to the run-round loop are in the foreground. *J. Tarrant/Kidderminster Railway Museum*

Through coaches were restored between Waterloo and Lyme Regis on summer Saturdays from 1950 but from 14th January, 1951 the Sunday services were cancelled for almost three months because of a coal shortage and when re-instated on 1st April only four trains ran in each direction, the late afternoon and evening services being covered by Southern National buses, which as previously used the more direct route between the two towns and omitted serving Combpyne. The journey time by rail was 21 minutes and by bus 26 minutes. The timetable was:

Down

										sn
Weekdays		am	am	pm	pm	pm	pm	pm	pm	pm	pm
Axminster	dep.	8.35	10.40	12.02	1.05	2.00	2.55	4.43	5.40	8.55	9.45
Combpyne	dep.	8.47	10.52	12.14	1.17	2.12	3.07	4.55	5.52	9.07	–
Lyme Regis	arr.	8.56	11.01	12.23	1.26	2.21	3.16	5.04	6.01	9.16	10.11

		Sundays				sn
		am	pm	pm	pm	pm
Axminster	dep.	11.11	12.40	2.48	4.25	8.40
Combpyne	dep.	11.23	12.52	3.00	4.37	–
Lyme Regis	arr.	11.32	1.01	3.09	4.46	9.06

Up

		sn									
Weekdays		am	am	am	am	pm	pm	pm	pm	pm	pm	pm
Lyme Regis	dep.	7.15	8.04	10.00	11.34	12.29	1.31	2.26	3.55	5.10	6.07	8.22
Combpyne	dep.	–	8.12	10.08	11.42	12.37	1.39	2.34	4.03	5.18	6.15	8.30
Axminster	arr.	7.40	8.25	10.21	11.55	12.50	1.52	2.47	4.16	5.31	6.28	8.43

		Sundays				sn	sn	sn
		am	am	pm	pm	pm	pm	pm
Lyme Regis	dep	10.40	11.37	2.13	3.55	4.59	6.04	7.26
Combpyne	dep	10.48	11.45	2.21	4.03	–	–	–
Axminster	arr	11.01	11.58	2.34	4.16	5.30	6.35	7.52

sn – Southern National bus

The 1953 summer passenger timetable showed a Monday to Friday service of nine trains in each direction augmented to 11 each way on Saturdays and nine each way on Sundays. The Saturday service included through coaches from and to London, the down stock being attached to the rear of 10.45 am ex-Waterloo, whilst in the up direction the coaches departed Lyme Regis at 2.35 pm and were attached to the 2.20 pm ex-Seaton at Axminster for onward transit to Waterloo, and at 3.05 pm for attaching to the 12.45 pm ex-Torrington to Waterloo.

In 1957 the service had again been reduced and Lyme Regis departures were 7.15 SN bus, 8.11, 10.08, 11.37 am. 1.10, 2.06, 3.55, 5.10, 6.07 and 8.22 pm, whilst from Axminster trains departed at 8.45, 10.40 am, 12.53, 1.38, 2.38, 4.42, 5.40, 6.07, 8.55 and 9.45 pm SN bus. On Sundays four trains ran in each direction after which Southern National buses covered the service.

The passenger traffic on the branch was essentially local in character boosted on Thursdays by extra demand for passenger travelling to Axminster market. The small regular flow of holidaymakers throughout the year increased considerably during the summer months when family holidaymakers swelled the population of the area.

'415' class No. 30584 approaches Combpyne and is passing over the entry points to the siding at the back of the platform. In the background is New Road overbridge No. 14 at 4 miles 31 chains.
Ivo Peters

Adams Radial tank No. 30584 makes heavy weather of her single-coach train as she departs Combpyne for Lyme Regis. *R.C Riley*

Despite being high summer '415' class No. 30584 pauses at Combpyne with only a single-coach branch train on 7th July, 1959. Note the back of the platform has been reduced to a grassy bank, with the former loop converted to a siding occupied by a camping coach.   *H.C. Casserley*

'415' class No. 30582 backs on to the single-coach Lyme Regis branch train in the bay platform at Axminster on 25th May, 1956. The coach was deliberately left at the top end of the platform to allow the locomotive to run-round the train after the up arrival. Note the large water storage tank above the pump house by the buffer stops with its associated tall chimney, a notable landmark in the area.   *H.B. Priestley*

'415' class No. 30582 approaching Combpyne with a three-coach down train in 1957. The leading vehicle is the through coach from Waterloo to Lyme Regis and the remaining stock the two-coach branch set. *R.J. Leonard/Kidderminster Railway Museum*

'415' class No. 30582 rouses the echoes as she departs Combpyne with a Lyme Regis to Axminster train in August 1957. The train has just passed over Combpyne Farm underbridge No. 13. In the left background is the camping coach stabled in the siding at the back of Combpyne platform. *R.J. Leonard/Kidderminster Railway Museum*

The normal load for trains during the winter months was one coach whilst summer services, Saturdays excepted, were usually formed of two coaches.

An interesting working existed for many years, on summer Saturdays, when the branch locomotives were changed over and some trains were hauled by two locomotives. The day began with the relieving locomotive running light from Exmouth Junction shed to Axminster in order to pilot the first down passenger train to Lyme Regis. On arrival at Lyme Regis home signal the leading engine was detached to run forward into the main platform. The remaining engine then hauled the two coach train into the bay platform where passengers alighted. The train was then shunted by the first engine on to the four through coaches destined for London Waterloo, which had been standing in the main platform. Thus released, the branch engine then coupled to the front of the first engine and double-headed the train back to Axminster. This operation called for smart station working and was often accomplished in seven minutes. On arrival at Axminster the four through coaches for London were taken by the branch engine into the up main line transfer siding and attached to an Exeter to Waterloo train, whilst the relieving engine returned to Lyme Regis with the two-coach branch train. The branch locomotive then waited at Axminster for the first through coaches from Waterloo detached off a through train to Exmouth. After the departure of the down main line train the three or four through coaches to Lyme Regis were shunted over to the up side into the main line transfer siding until the return of the branch train, when both locomotives double-headed the combined branch train and through coaches to Lyme Regis. Both locomotives were then utilized to haul the return two-coach branch train to Axminster, where one was detached to await another through train from Waterloo whilst the other made a round trip from Axminster to Lyme Regis with the branch train. With the arrival of the through train from Waterloo to Seaton at Axminster the five through coaches to Lyme Regis were detached and worked double-headed as a complete train to Lyme Regis usually arriving just after 2.00 pm. The complete train then forming a return through service from Lyme Regis to Waterloo was worked as far as Axminster by the two locomotives. At Axminster the five coaches were coupled to a Torrington to Waterloo train and the double heading was completed for another summer Saturday. The retiring locomotive was then worked back to Exmouth Junction shed, whilst the fresh branch locomotive was left to handle all services for the following week. Although enjoying these through services to and from Waterloo, Lyme Regis was never honoured with a through coach attached to the 'Atlantic Coast Express'.

Specific instructions were issued for trains hauled by two engines coupled together. At Axminster when it was necessary for the leading engine to be detached before the train entered the up bay line, so that it was available for shunting purposes, the shunter was required to bring the train to a stand on the approach side of No. 6 points by the exhibition of a red hand signal in accordance with rule 50 (a). The shunter, after obtaining the Train Staff or Tablet from the driver of the train engine had to accompany the leading engine to the bay platform and then convey the Train Staff or Tablet to the signalman. When the leading engine had proceeded to the up siding and No. 6 points had been returned to their normal position, the train was hand signalled into the bay platform. At Lyme Regis, when it was necessary for the leading engine of a train hauled by two engines to be detached before entering the station, similarly the train was to be brought to a stand at No. 3 shunt signal by the exhibition of a red hand signal. The shunter then had to obtain the Train Staff or Tablet from the driver of the train engine and after the leading

WEEKDAYS   LYME REGIS BRANCH   G 87

These timings WILL NOT APPLY ON SATURDAYS, 17th June to 9th September, 1961

Mileage M	Mileage C	DOWN		am	am	Run as Mixed Train when required	PM	PM	Commences 11th Sept.	PM	Until 8th Sept. inclusive	PM	Commences 11th Sept.	PM	Until 8th Sept. inclusive		PM	PM	PM		PM
0	0	AXMINSTER © dep	1	8 45	10 32		12 33	1 38		1 48		2 40		2 48		..	4 36	5 40	6 47	..	8 55
4	21	Combpyne	2	8 58	10 45		12 46	1 51		2 1		2 53		3 1		..	4 49	5 53	7 0	..	9 8
6	59	LYME REGIS © arr	3	9 5½	10 52½		12 53½	1 58½		2 8½		3 0½		3 8½		..	4 56½	6 0½	7 7½	..	9 15½

Mileage M	Mileage C	UP		am	am	Mixed		am		PM	PM	Commences 11th Sept.	PM	Until 8th Sept. inclusive		PM		PM
0	0	LYME REGIS © dep	1	8 11	9 45		..	11 40	..	1 8	2 6		2 16		..	3 53	..	5 10
2	38	Combpyne	2	8 19½	9 53½		..	11 48½	..	1 16½	2 14½		2 24½		..	4 1½	..	5 18½
6	59	AXMINSTER © arr	3	8 32	10 6		..	12 1	..	1 29	2 27		2 37		..	4 14	..	5 31

			PM		PM					
LYME REGIS .. dep	1	6 10	..	8 22	..	..	..	..	..	..
Combpyne	2	6 18½	..	8 30½	..	..	..	..	..	..
AXMINSTER .. arr	3	6 31	..	8 43	..	..	..	..	..	..

SATURDAYS These timings WILL APPLY ON SATURDAYS, 17th June to 9th September, 1961

DOWN

		am		am	am	am	PM		PM	PM	Through coaches from Waterloo	PM	PM	PM	PM
AXMINSTER .. dep	1	8 10	..	9 35	10 40	11 39	12 43	..	1 55	2 8		2 15½	4 42	5 42	6 50	8 55
Combpyne	2	8 23	..	9 48	10 53	11 52	12 56	..	2 8	3 13½		5 2½	4 55	5 55	7 3	9 8
LYME REGIS .. arr	3	8 30½	..	9 55½	11 0½	11 59½	1 3½	..	2 15½			5 2½	6 2½	7 10½	9 15½

UP

		am	am		am	am	PM	PM	PM	Through coaches for Waterloo	PM	PM	PM
LYME REGIS .. dep	1	7 35	8 50	..	10 10	11 8	12 10	1 14	3 5		5 10	6 12	8 22
Combpyne	2	7 43½	8 58½	..	10 18½	11 16½	12 18½	1 22½	3 13½		5 18½	6 20½	8 30½
AXMINSTER .. arr	3	7 56	9 11	..	10 31	11 29	12 31	1 35	3 26	..	5 31	6 33	8 43

SUNDAYS Until 10th September, 1961, inclusive

DOWN

		am	PM		PM	PM		PM	PM	PM	PM	PM	Exen. No. 263 PM Runs 2nd & 16th July and 13th August only
AXMINSTER .. dep	1	11 6	12 14	..	1 14	2 30	..	3 37	5 48	7 16	8 18	9 28	10 34
Combpyne	2	11 19	12 27	..	1 27	2 43	..	3 50	6 1	7 29	8 31	9 41	10 47
LYME REGIS .. arr	3	11 26½	12 34½	..	1 34½	2 50½	..	3 57½	6 8½	7 36½	8 38½	9 48½	10 54½

UP

		am	am		PM	PM	PM		PM	PM		PM	Exen. No. 263 PM Available for ordinary passengers Runs 2nd & 16th July and 13th August only
LYME REGIS .. dep	1	10 25	11 34	..	12 42	1 50	3 0	..	5 10	6 36	7 44	..	8 50	10 0
Combpyne	2	10 33½	11 42½	..	12 50½	1 58½	3 8½	..	5 18½	6 44½	7 52½	..	8 58½	10 8½
AXMINSTER .. arr	3	10 46	11 55	..	1 3	2 11	3 21	..	5 31	6 57	8 5	..	9 11	10 21

BR(SR) working timetable June 1961.

engine had been admitted to the yard under authority of No. 3 shunt signal, the signal had to be replaced to the 'on' position, and then lowered again after the route had been set up, for the train to enter the platform.

The freight timetable for 1963 showed an SX light engine movement departing Lyme Regis at 6.15 am arriving at Axminster at 6.30 am to return with the 7.29 am class '9' goods train ex-Axminster arriving Lyme Regis at 7.48 am. The 8.14 am mixed train from Axminster, calling at Combpyne 8.20½ to 8.21 am and arriving at Axminster at 8.32 am conveyed any additional wagons not taken by the earlier train. Equally the 10.32 am mixed train ex-Axminster ran as a 'Q' 'as and when required working' SX until 6th September and then every weekday from 9th September to convey stray wagons not conveyed by the earlier trains.

The summer timetable commencing in June 1964, operated by dmus and worked from the Axminster end of the line showed Monday to Friday departures from Axminster at 7.15, 8.08, 10.15 am, 12.30, 1.42, 2.45, 4.35, 5.40, 6.40 and 10.05 SN pm; Saturday departures at 7.15, 8.10, 10.35, 11.27 am, 12.15, 1 25, 2.25, 3.40, 4.35, 5.40, 6.05 and 10. 05 SN pm whilst Sunday services departed Axminster at 11.06 am, 12.10, 1.02, 2.10, 3.15, 4.30, 5.48, 7.16 and 8.25 pm. In the up direction Monday to Friday departures from Lyme Regis were 6.31 SN, 7.38, 9.45, 11.32 am, 1.10, 2.09, 4.05, 5.13, 6.10 and 7.02 pm; Saturday departures were 6.31 SN, 7.38, 9.45, 11.00, 11.50 am, 12.40, 1.48, 2.50, 4.02, 5.15, 6.10 and 7.25 pm whilst Sunday trains departed at 11.37 am, 12.31, 1.40, 2.45, 4.00, 5.13, 6.40, 7.45 and 8.50 pm. Southern National operated services are denoted by SN.

The final timetable allowed dmus 18 minutes for the journey and trains departed Lyme Regis at 7.38, 9.52, 10.40, 11.44 am, 12.40, 1.29, 2.40, 3.39, 5.17, 6.22 and 7.10 pm and from Axminster 7.15, 8.05, 10.15, 11.15 am, 12.15, 1.03, 2.19, 3.05, 4.10, 5.45 and 6.48 pm. The first down and last up trains ran from and to Exeter Central.

BR(WR) working timetable winter 1964.

Fares

The initial single fares from Axminster to Lyme Regis on the opening of the line was third class 6½d., first class 9½d., and from Waterloo to Lyme Regis £1 5s. 1d. first class, 15s. 9d. second class and 12s. 7d. third class

In 1910 tourist, weekly and fortnightly excursion tickets were issued from London Waterloo and other principal LSWR stations during the summer months, whilst weekend tickets, available from Fridays to Tuesdays, were issued at reduced rates. The 1914 summer tourist return ticket prices from London Waterloo to Lyme Regis were: first class £2 3s. 0d.; second class £1 7s. 6d .; third class £1 4s. 3d.

As second-class accommodation was not provided on the branch, second class fare paying passengers were up-graded to travel first class.

Just before the outbreak of World War II the third class single fare between Axminster and Lyme Regis was 11d., whilst in 1951 the local third class fare structure was:

		s.	d.
Single	Lyme Regis to Combpyne	0	6
	Lyme Regis to Axminster	1	5
	Combpyne to Axminster		11½
Monthly return	Lyme Regis to Combpyne	1	0
	Lyme Regis to Axminster	2	2

By 1947 fares from Waterloo to the branch stations were:

	1st single	1st return	3rd single	3rd return
Axminster	42s. 0d.	51s. 0d.	25s. 5d.	34s. 0d.
Combpyne	43s. 8d.	52s. 6d.	26s. 3d.	35s. 0d.
Lyme Regis	44s. 4d.	53s. 6d.	26s. 7d.	35s. 8d.

In the 1955 there had been an appreciable reduction in single fares but a significant increase in returns:

	1st single	1st return	3rd single	3rd return
Axminster	34s. 2d.	68s. 4d.	22s. 9d.	45s. 6d.
Combpyne	35s. 5d.	70s. 10d.	23s. 7d.	47s. 2d.
Lyme Regis	35s. 9d.	71s. 6d.	23s. 10d.	47s. 8d.

By 1962 a sample of second class ordinary and mid-week period reduced return fares to Lyme Regis were:

	Ordinary			Mid-week		
	£	s.	d.	£	s.	d.
London	3	10	0	2	13	0
Birmingham Snow Hill	3	15	0	2	17	0
Bradford	6	2	0	4	11	6
Cambridge	4	16	0	3	12	0
Cardiff General	2	11	0	1	19	0
Derby	4	18	0	3	14	0
Edinburgh Waverley	9	2	0	6	17	0
Glasgow Central	9	2	0	6	17	0

	Ordinary			Mid-week		
	£	s.	d.	£	s.	d.
Hull	6	6	0	4	14	6
Leeds City	5	18	0	4	8	6
Liverpool	5	10	0	4	3	0
Manchester	5	0	8	4	3	0
Newcastle upon Tyne	7	12	0	5	14	0
Norwich	5	12	0	4	4	0
Nottingham	5	0	0	3	15	0
Preston	5	12	0	4	4	0
Sheffield	5	8	0	4	1	0
Stafford	4	11	0	3	9	0
Swansea High Street	3	12	0	2	14	0
Wolverhampton Low Level	4	1	0	3	1	0

The single fares in 1964 from London Waterloo were:

	1st single	2nd single
Axminster	54s. 5d.	36s. 3d.
Combpyne	56s. 3d.	37s. 6d.
Lyme Regis	57s. 0d.	38s. 0d.

Holiday season tickets were initially issued by the LSWR and these continued through the Southern era. By 1962 the Lyme Regis branch was included in Holiday Runabout Ticket areas 12 and 14, the former including an area stretching from Exeter Central and Exmouth in the west to Chard town via Chard Junction in the east whilst area 14 extended from Sidmouth in the west to Sherborne and Yeovil Pen Mill in the east and Thornfalcon and Martock to the north; both priced at 21s. 0d. for seven days travel and valid from 29th April to 27th October.

On busy summer Saturdays one of the signalmen at Axminster was booked on duty to collect tickets from passengers travelling on the branch to save congestion at Lyme Regis. He was also responsible for ensuring the toilets of coaching stock on through trains to and from Waterloo were replenished with soap and toilet rolls.

Goods traffic

Unfortunately Lyme Regis had little industry other than the holiday trade and freight traffic consisted almost entirely of incoming merchandise. In the early years most trains ran as mixed and conveyed wagon loads as and when received at Axminster or when emptied at Lyme Regis, but in later years the branch locomotive departed Lyme Regis at 6.15 am and travelled light engine to pick up the daily freight, which shunted the siding at Combpyne and at the same time cleared the station of empty wagons. One mixed train was permitted in each direction and this enabled empty wagons or outgoing traffic to be cleared from Lyme Regis. Freight traffic consisted mainly of coal, corn, cement, bricks, slag, fertilizer and smalls traffic for local shops, whilst a small amount of cattle and sheep traffic, the latter from Combpyne, was conveyed en route to and from local markets at Chard and Exeter.

Milk was conveyed in the familiar 17 gallon churns, latterly mostly to the United Dairies depot at Chard Junction but in the decade before closure of the line the commodity was conveyed direct from farm by road. A regular consignee for van load traffic was Boots the Chemist with a wagon arriving each week from Beeston, Nottingham.

Down freight trains were not allowed to exceed 12 wagons in length, whilst in the up direction a load of 15 wagons was permitted. When the down train reached Lyme Regis down home signal it was the practice for the engine to be detached and run forward before the wagons were released to run by gravity down the 1 in 240 gradient into the sidings, a practice not permitted with coaching stock. Most commodities other than coal were handled in the goods shed and off-loaded by the 1 ton 5 cwt, later 15 cwt, capacity fixed crane.

Coal and coke was regularly brought to Combpyne and Lyme Regis for domestic and horticultural purposes and five fuel merchants served the area: Bradford & Sons, J.P. Moore, Brown & Rattenbury, W.H. Pinney & Co. and W.H. Thomas & Sons.

A small amount of fish traffic was dispatched from Lyme Regis in the halcyon days including Lyme Bay sole and mackerel usually loaded in the passenger brake van, much to the displeasure of the guard. He also had to endure incoming supplies of fish including cod, haddock and herring for the local fishmonger and hotels. Especially malodorous were the smoked kippers from as far away as Yarmouth and Scotland when the scent seemed to last for days in the offending brake van.

All Hallows School at Rousden used the railway facilities for many years for the dispatch and receipt of pupil's luggage at the beginning and end of each term. Outgoing luggage was amassed at the school and taken to Lyme Regis station where three covered vans were stabled in the bay platform and loaded, one being sent to Exeter, one to Salisbury and the third to Nine Elms, London. Some of this traffic was also routed via Combpyne. Return luggage came piecemeal via normal passenger or goods services.

Freight facilities were withdrawn from the line on and from 3rd February, 1964 and from Axminster on and from 18th April, 1966.

The following goods facilities were available at the branch stations:

Axminster	Loading gauges	
	Fixed crane	4 ton 11 cwt capacity
	Goods shed	
	Goods office	
	Loading dock	
	Cattle dock	
	Wagon weighbridge	
	Cart weighbridge	
	Stables	
Combpyne	Loading gauge	
	Loading dock	
Lyme Regis	Loading gauge	
	Fixed crane	1 ton 5 cwt capacity (with 12 ft 2 in. height of lift) later reduced to 15 cwt capacity
	Goods shed	
	Loading dock	
	Cattle dock	

Chapter Eight

Locomotives and Rolling Stock

The 12 tons axle load limit of the new light railway severely restricted the choice of motive power available to the LSWR to work the line. During construction work the main line company made available to the contractor a Beyer, Peacock & Co. '330' class saddle tank No. 131 dating from 1882 (Works No. 2127), 'because of the steepness of the gradients and severity of the curves' and at first it was considered that locomotives of the '330' class might work the services. The leading dimensions of the class were:

Cylinders	2 inside	17 in. x 24 in.
Motion		Stephenson with slide valves
Boiler		
Length		9 ft 4 in.
Diameter		4 ft 0 in.
Firebox		4 ft 7 in.
Heating surface		
Tubes		824.6 sq. ft
Firebox		76.7 sq. ft
Total		901.3 sq. ft
Grate area		14.0 sq. ft
Boiler pressure		130 psi
Coupled wheels		4 ft 1 in.
Wheelbase		13 ft 9 in.
Weight in working order		34 tons 19½ cwt
Max axle loading		12 tons 0 cwt
Water capacity		800 gallons

As difficulties were experienced with the '330' class Dugald Drummond, the LSWR mechanical engineer, then proposed to build two small 0-4-4 tank locomotives at Nine Elms, with 4 ft 6 in. coupled wheels, 14 in. by 24 in. cylinders and weighing approximately 30 tons 15 cwt, especially for the line. However, before the necessary action was taken the London Brighton & South Coast Railway offered some of their 'A1' class 0-6-0 'Terrier' tank locomotives for sale, and after inspection, two of the class, No. 646 *Newington* and No. 668 *Clapham*, were purchased in March 1903 for £500 each. No. 646 had run 574,266 miles since new in January 1877 and No. 668, 611,070 miles since entering service in August 1874. After further inspection and attention at Nine Elms works and the replacement of the Westinghouse air brake equipment with vacuum brake, they were repainted in LSWR green livery and renumbered 734 and 735 respectively and entered service in April 1903. After running-in duties at Guildford and Bournemouth depots they were sent to Exmouth Junction shed from where trial runs were made between Axminster and Lyme Regis in August before the pair worked the inaugural services.

Thereafter, except for busy periods, one 'Terrier' worked the branch whilst the other shunted in the Exeter area. By August 1905 the 0-6-0s were finding the heavier holiday services beyond their capabilities on the steep gradients and often an Exmouth Junction 'O2' class 0-4-4 tank locomotive was deputizing or assisting. The 'O2s', however, could only work over the branch with partially filled side tanks and bunker which somewhat

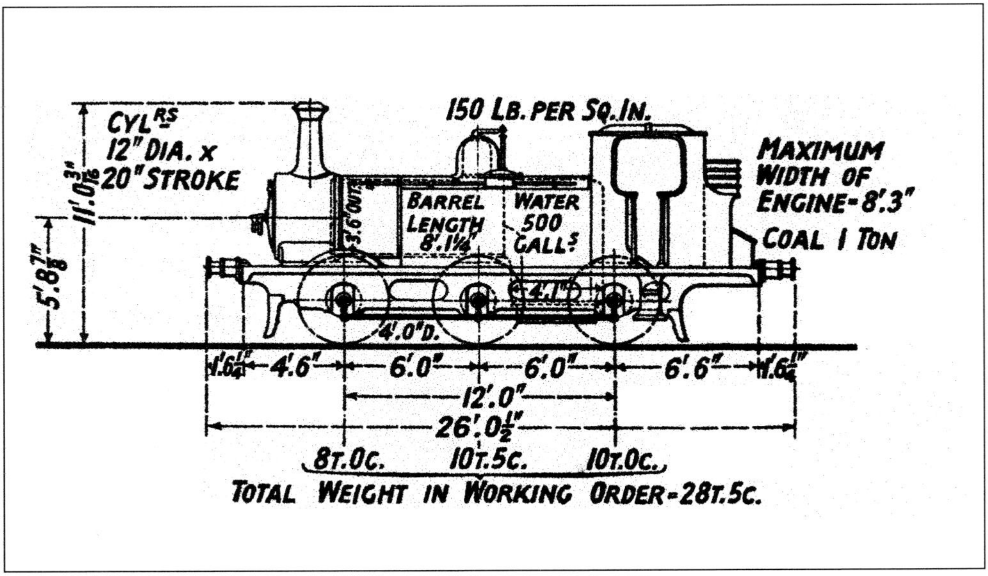

SR diagram of 'A1X' class 0-6-0T.

SR diagram of 'O2' class 0-4-4T.

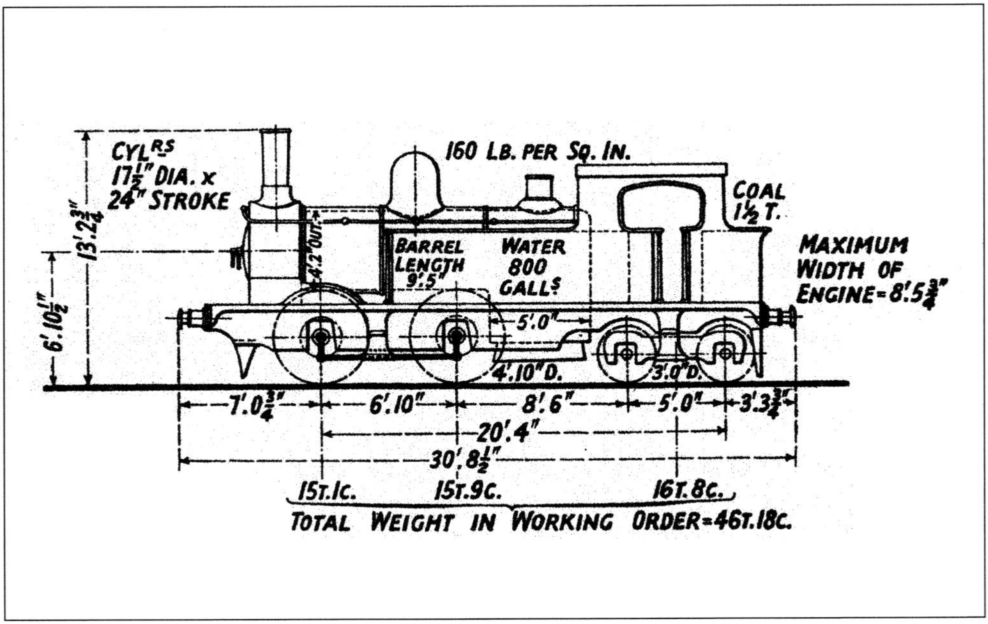

restricted availability. After the summer services Nos. 734 and 735 resumed their duties, but evidently not to the satisfaction of the LSWR authorities, for early in January 1906 'O2' class No 223 was sent to Lyme Regis for trials with side tanks marked to show the maximum permissible water capacity within the weight restrictions imposed on the line. The 'O2' proved successful and during the summer of 1906 it worked the services with 'Terrier' No. 735. Sister locomotive No. 734 was transferred away to Yeovil and subsequently sold to the Freshwater, Yarmouth & Newport Railway on the Isle of Wight in 1913, where it became their No. 2. It later passed to the SR who named it *Freshwater* and renumbered it W8. It returned to the mainland under British Railways, where it worked on the Hayling Island branch as No. 32646 until withdrawal in November 1963. The locomotive was sold to the owner of the Droxford to Fareham line but in 1966 it was sold to a brewery and was plinthed outside the 'Hayling Billy' public house on Hayling Island. The locomotive, restored as W8 *Freshwater*, is now on the Isle of Wight operating services on the preserved steam railway between Smallbrook and Wootton. For a short while No. 735 lingered on, occasionally working to Lyme Regis, but was then transferred away leaving the 'O2' class in sole charge. No. 735 was finally withdrawn by the SR in 1936, after working on the Plymouth Devonport & South Western Junction Railway and Lee-on-Solent Light Railway, the latter until closure in 1928. After this it was transferred to Ashford where it was used on various menial duties including a period of loan to Westenhanger colliery in 1932. It was fitted with an LSWR-style stovepipe chimney in 1920 and also fitted with pulley wheels on the cab roof for operating the LSWR system of rail motor control. On transfer to Ashford complete vacuum brake equipment was provided for working the locomotive brakes as well as those on the train.

LBSCR	LSWR	SR	BR	Withdrawn
No.	No.	Nos.	No.	
646 *Newington*	734	W2, W8, 2646	32646	November 1963
668 *Clapham*	735	2668		1936

The leading dimensions of the 'A1' class were,

Cylinders		13 in. x 20 in. (No. 735)
		14 in. x 20 in. (No. 734)
Motion		Stephenson with slide valves
Heating surface		
Tubes	121 x 1¾ in.	453 sq ft
Firebox		53 sq. ft
Total		506 sq ft
Coupled wheels		4 ft 0 in.
Wheelbase		12 ft 0 in.
Boiler		
Length		7 ft 10 in.
Diameter		3 ft 6 in.
Firebox		4 ft 1 in.
Grate area		11.25 sq. ft
Boiler pressure		150 psi
Water capacity		500 gallons
Coal capacity		1 ton
Weight in working order		24 tons 12 cwt
Tractive effort		7,650 lb.

The 'Terriers' resumed duties on the branch for the remainder of the winter months (1906) but as conditions improved and trains were strengthened No. 228 was again outbased at Lyme Regis. By May 1907 Exmouth Junction shed had allocated three 'O2' class engines, Nos. 177, 202 and 228 to the Lyme Regis branch duties with one working the branch passenger and freight services and the others working elsewhere in the Exeter district. The three locomotives were augmented by No. 223 in 1911 and utilized until 1913/14 by which time continued use on the sharply curved line had caused excessive flange wear and distorted frames. The continuous damage to both locomotives and track forced the LSWR authorities to seek alternative motive power. During World War II 'O2' No. 199 deputized on the branch on several occasions when the 4-4-2Ts were under repair, but on one occasion derailed outside of Lyme Regis station. Locomotives associated with the branch were:

LSWR No.	SR No.	BR No.	Withdrawn
177	177	30177	October 1959
184	184/W27	W27 *Merstone*	December 1966
199	199	30199	December 1962
202	202/W29	W29 *Alverstone*	May 1966
223	223	30223	October 1961
227	227	–	June 1933
228	228	–	August 1943
230	230	30230	July 1956

The principal dimensions of the 'O2' class were,

Cylinders	17½ in. x 24 in.
	17 in. x 24 in. (No. 177)
Motion	Stephenson with slide valves
Heating surface	
Tubes	898.0 sq. ft
Firebox	89.0 sq. ft
Total	987.0 sq. ft
Coupled wheels	4 ft 10 in.
Trailing wheels	3 ft 0 in.
Wheelbase	20 ft 4 in.
Coupled wheelbase	6 ft 10 in.
Boiler	
Diameter	4 ft 2 in.
Length	9 ft 5 in.
Firebox	5 ft 0 in.
Grate area	13.83 sq. ft
Boiler pressure	160 psi
Water capacity	800 gallons
Coal capacity	1 ton 10 cwt
Max. axle weight	15 tons 5 cwt
Weight in working order	44 tons 15½ cwt
Tractive effort	17,245 lb.

The answer to the 'O2 class problem lay in the ageing Adams '415' class 4-4-2 tank locomotives built by four different manufacturers for suburban and branch passenger work, which by 1900 were displaced from their original duties and mostly on the duplicate list by having '0' added before the running number. After modification to give the bogie and radial truck greater side play to ease the negotiation of the 5½ chain radius curves No. 0125, which had been built by Robert Stephenson & Co. in September 1885 (Works No. 2608), left Eastleigh works and ran trials between Axminster and Lyme Regis with both passenger and freight trains on 16th October, 1913. Although considered adequate the civil engineer required the locomotive to run with only 800 gallons of water in the side tanks, 27 inches from the bottom, instead of the normal 1,000 gallons, to reduce axle loading. So successful was the performance over the 'O2' class that in the New Year two similarly modified locomotives were drafted to work on the line. No. 521 arrived in mid-March 1914 and No. 0419 in November of the same year. No. 521 had been built by Dübs & Co. in December 1885 (Works No. 2110), whilst No. 0419 dated from September 1882 and was built by Beyer, Peacock (Works No. 2171). Based at Exmouth Junction, one locomotive was utilized on the Lyme Regis branch whilst the others found duties on passenger services on the Exeter to Exmouth branch, Sidmouth Junction to Sidmouth branch and the Seaton Junction to Seaton line - the changeover for the Lyme Regis branch normally taking place on Saturday afternoon. During the summer months two locomotives were normally required with one spare and it was possible to cover routine maintenance without having to resort to using 'O2' class engines. All three retained their LSWR green paintwork until No. 0419 was laid aside in March 1921 and replaced by No. 0486 built in March 1885 by Neilson & Co. (Works No. 3207). No. 0419 was withdrawn from traffic in November 1921 to be followed by No 0521 in July 1925. No. 0125 was thus left to handle all the branch traffic with No. 0486 until February 1926 when another modified '415' class No. 0520. originally built by Dübs & Co. in December 1885 (Works No. 2109), arrived to assist. Despite the use of these three locomotives, Exmouth Junction 'O2' class tank locomotives still made occasional visits, when one or other of the 4-4-2Ts was undergoing boiler washout or maintenance. In January 1928 No. 0486 was withdrawn from traffic and by October 1928 difficulties were experienced when the two 4-4-2 tank engines required heavy maintenance, but before monetary authorization for repairs to such aged machines was sanctioned alternative motive power had to be sought.

The SR authorities were loath to re-employ the 'O2' class on a long term basis and so alternatives arrived for trials in the form of ex-South Eastern & Chatham Railway (SECR) 'P' class 0-6-0 tank locomotive No. A558 dating from June 1910 and former London Brighton & South Coast Railway 'D1' class 0-4-2 tank locomotive No. B612. Each worked the branch traffic for one week. The 'P' class having ventured westward in the summer of 1928 for trials on the Wenfordbridge clay line in Cornwall, where it failed miserably, was on the return journey tried on the Lyme Regis branch, where it disgraced itself for being totally underpowered and lost time on most journeys, even with one coach.

SECR No.	SR No.	BR No.	Withdrawn
558	A558/1558	31558	February 1960

The 'D1' class, however, with reduced coal and water competently tackled the grades and curves on the branch and four locomotives were subsequently transferred to Exmouth Junction to take over the branch workings, but before entering service their weight had to be reduced to satisfy the civil engineer. Nos. B276 and B633 were taken into Brighton works to have their weight reduced to a figure acceptable to the civil engineer. The bunker was cut down and the tank capacity restricted to 580 gallons, which gave a maximum weight of 41 tons 6 cwt 14

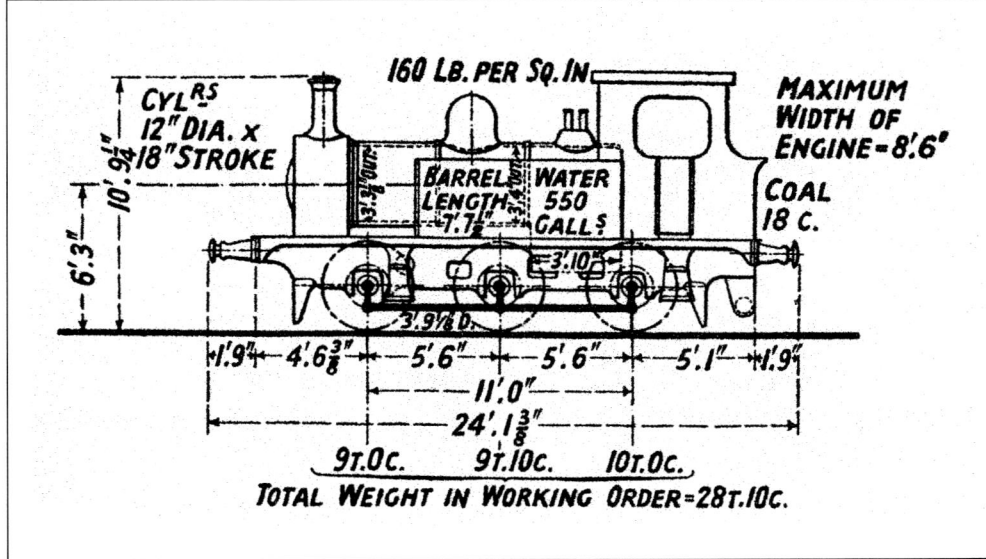

SR diagram of 'P' class 0-6-0T.

'D1' class 0-4-2T No. B633 shown on steam heating duties at Exmouth Junction shed in July 1938. The engine was one of four delegated to work the Lyme Regis branch, hence the cut down bunker to reduce weight, but all were abject failures. Under the SR renumbering scheme of 1931 the 'B' designating Brighton should have been removed as all ex-LBSC locomotives had 2000 added to their fleet number but when scrapped in February 1944 the engine still carried her old number.   *R.C. Riley Collection*

quarters, 14 cwt within the limit. When returned to traffic in March and April 1929 they were sent to Exmouth Junction for trials on the Lyme Regis branch and as these appeared successful. Nos. B359 and B612 were similarly modified in Brighton works in September and July 1929. The locomotives not required to work the Lyme Regis line were utilized on the neighbouring Sidmouth branch and carriage shunting at Exeter. Within months of taking over the branch services the 'D1s' were suffering a similar fate as the 'O2s', with leaking tubes, loose tyres and strained frames brought about by the severe gradients and sharp curves on the line. In wet weather the position was exacerbated, as the class was prone to slipping causing excessive flange wear. By April 1930 Nos. B276 and B359 were unserviceable because of strained frames and leaking tanks whilst No. B633 was away at Eastleigh works receiving general overhaul leaving only No. B612 available for traffic working alongside an 'O2' class engine. The local enginemen thus petitioned for the return of the two Adams 4-4-2Ts. Details of the 'D1' class follow:

LBSCR No.	SR 1st No.	SR 2nd No.	Withdrawn
276 *Rudgewick*	B276	2276	December 1935
359 *Egmont*	B359	2359	July 1951
612 *Wallington*	B612	2612	October 1934 *
633 *Mitcham*	B633	2633	February 1944 †

* Originally LBSCR No. 12. † Originally LBSCR No. 33.

The principal dimensions of the 'D1' class were:

Cylinders	17 in. x 24 in.
Motion	Stephenson with slide valves
Heating surface	
Tubes	845.0 sq. ft
Firebox	88.0 sq. ft
Total	933.0 sq. ft
Coupled wheels	5 ft 6 in.
Trailer wheels	4 ft 6 in.
Wheelbase	15 ft 0 in.
Coupled wheelbase	7 ft 7 in.
Boiler	
Diameter	4 ft 0 in.
Length	10 ft 2 in.
Firebox	5 ft 2¼ in.
Grate area	15.25 sq. ft
Boiler pressure	140 psi
Water capacity	580 gallons
Coal capacity	1 ton
Max. axle loading	14 tons 11 cwt
Weight in working order	41 tons 6 cwt
Tractive effort	15,200 lb.

In the meantime in the absence of financial authority for repairs the two Adams '415' class locomotives had been laid aside and tallowed down at Exmouth Junction shed pending removal to Eastleigh works for scrapping. The daily reports of the poor performance of the 'D1' class and a request from local staff for the retention of the 4-4-2Ts

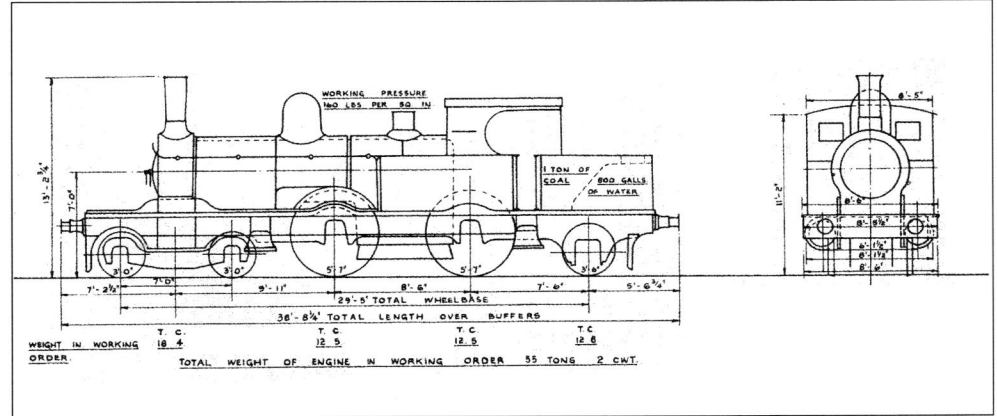

LSWR diagram of '415' class 4-4-2T.

East Kent Railway No. 5 formerly LSWR '415' class 4-4-2T No 488, later 0488 built by Neilson & Co. in 1885. Surplus to requirements it was sold in September 1917 for service at the Royal Navy Salvage Depot Ridham Dock before being transferred to the Government General Stores Depot at Belvedere two years later. Again redundant it was purchased by the East Kent Railway in April 1921 and served on that line until the outbreak of World War II. The SR desperate for suitable motive power to strengthen the fleet of two Radial tanks on the Lyme Regis branch sought and purchased the derelict locomotive in March 1946 for £120. It was thoroughly overhauled and emerged from Eastleigh works as No 3488, then becoming No. 30583 under nationalization. *Author's Collection*

resulted in the pair being reprieved and both received a thorough overhaul at Eastleigh in 1930; the work including provision of new frames, cylinders, fireboxes, springs, tyres and well tanks. No. 0125 entered works on 17th March and was released to traffic on 24th July whilst No. 0520 went to works on 17th April and was released to traffic on 14th August; the extensive improvements costing £1,290 and £1,330 respectively. By August both were back at Exmouth Junction and working turn and turn about at Lyme Regis leaving the 0-4-2 tank engines to be dispersed elsewhere on the Southern system. No. 0125, painted Maunsell green in July 1926, was renumbered 3125 in November 1933 and 0520, painted Maunsell green in January 1925, became 3520 in January 1934. The pair reigned supreme until 1946, except for few occasions during World War I when 'O2' class No 199 deputized. In January 1940 No. 3520 was painted Maunsell green with Bulleid lettering and numerals, but became plain black with Bulleid lettering and numerals in March 1945. No. 3125 was painted plain black with Bulleid lettering and numerals in November 1941. It was usually possible to schedule general repairs for the winter months so that at least one could maintain services on the branch, with assistance from an 'O2' class engine. However, after the war both were withdrawn for heavy repairs and the SR again resorted to employing 'O2s' on the branch, whilst the authorities sorted out the dilemma. It was evident that two locomotives were insufficient to cover all contingencies so the East Kent Railway (EKR) was approached for the purchase of their No. 5, ex-LSWR '415' class No. 488, later 0488, built by Neilson & Co. in March 1885 (Works No. 3209), which had been sold to the Royal Navy General Salvage Depot, Ridham Dock, in September 1917 for £2,105. After services at Ridham near Sittingbourne in Kent where it was No. 27, it was transferred to the Government General Stores Depot at Belvedere in late 1919 before being declared surplus to requirements and was purchased by Colonel Stephens for £800 for use on the East Kent Railway, entering service in April 1921. After service with the EKR, during which time it received repairs at the SR Ashford works, it was laid aside. Despite laying derelict since 1939 the locomotive was thought to be repairable and was bought by the SR for £120 in March 1946. After complete overhaul at Eastleigh works costing £1,638 the locomotive was taken into SR stock in August 1946 as No. 3488, being returned to traffic on 30th November painted plain black but the engine did not enter service on the Lyme Regis branch until the following month.

At nationalization all three locomotives passed to BR stock and were renumbered; No. 3125 became 30582 in March 1949, 3488 became 30583 in October 1949 both in lined black livery whilst 3520 became 30584 in April 1948 in plain black livery, ultimately receiving lined black in May 1951. The trio soldiered on for over a decade, but with ageing machines a replacement was always being sought. A welcome return to the branch was made, however, in 1953 by a 'Terrier' 0-6-0T when No. 32662 double-headed the Railway Correspondence & Travel Society's 24th Anniversary special train with No. 30583; No. 32646 old LSWR No. 734 had been requested but failed to make the journey.

With an average of 110,000 miles between shopping the three Adams tank locomotives were quickly reaching the end of their life, despite few failures in traffic. A replacement was imperative and after extensive track renewals on the branch in the summer of 1960 a London Midland '2MT' class 2-6-2 tank locomotive No. 41297 of Barnstaple shed was given trials over the light railway on Sunday 18th September. LMR '2MTs' had recently replaced the ageing 'M7' class 0-4-4Ts on local services in north Devon. A motive power inspector from Exmouth Junction shed and a Southern Region headquarters engineer from Brighton accompanied the crew. On the first down run the locomotive hauled an unfitted brake van only stopping at various places en

'415' class No. 30583 has passed Lyme Regis home signal and is approaching the terminus with the single-coach 1.38 pm train from Axminster on 14th July, 1955. The line in the foreground led to the bay platform. *LCGB/Ken Nunn*

Radial tank No. 30583 fitted with Drummond boiler incorporating the safety valves in the dome standing at Lyme Regis. The locomotive in early BR lined-black livery has the 'lion and wheel' emblem on the side tanks. *Author's Collection*

Waiting departure at Axminster; '415' class No. 30583 stands in the bay platform with the single-coach 12.38 pm train to Lyme Regis on 14th July, 1955. *LCGB/Ken Nunn*

A close up of '415' class 4-4-2T No 30584 standing at Lyme Regis platform showing the large bunker, with prominent water filler, square cab spectacles and small side tanks. The branch headcode of one white disc is carried in the centre of the buffer beam.
J. Tarrant/Kidderminster Railway Museum

Ground signal No. 12 is cleared to allow Radial tank No. 30583 to pass over No. 11 points and run round her train composed of two-coach set No. 108 at Lyme Regis in the early 1950s.

Oakwood Collection

On 28th February, 1965 LMR '2MT' No. 41206 leaks steam in the wintry air at Lyme Regis.

Author

route for clearance tests before pausing at Combpyne. The 2-6-2T then backed cautiously into the siding before moving forward into the dock road watched by the locomotive inspector. The engine then reversed into the siding and ran forward through the facing points back on to the main single line. No. 41297 then worked forward to Lyme Regis with occasional stops to check clearances before the brake van was left in one of the sidings. Clearances were checked in all sidings but the engine could not enter the engine shed as it was occupied by one of the Radial tank engines. The 2-6-2T then worked two Maunsell corridor passenger coaches from Lyme Regis to Axminster and back before again being tested in the sidings, with no problems occurring. After depositing the coaches No. 41297 returned light engine to Axminster and thence to Exmouth Junction.

The trials were promising and further tests were made on Sunday 13th November, 1960, when the branch was made available all day. No. 41308 arrived to double-head a three-coach train with Adams tank No. 30583. However the motive power inspector decided the 4-4-2T was not initially required as he wished to see the performance of the 2-6-2T with four coaches. With dew on the rails No 41308 slipped occasionally but Lyme Regis was reached without further incident and on return to Axminster the load was increased to five coaches. This load was easily handled with the locomotive barking up the 1 in 40 gradients to Combpyne and then drifting down to Lyme Regis. After successfully negotiating the branch No. 41308 then hauled six coaches unaided and proved master of its train again reaching Lyme Regis without incident. The 4-4-2T had been allowed to follow with her three-coach train and despite falling boiler pressure made Combpyne but it was evident the Adams engine was well past its best and she was allowed to roll downhill to Lyme Regis. At the conclusion of the trials the ex-LMR 2-6-2Ts were initially only permitted to work across the branch in an emergency but from the end of December 1960, and after further slight adjustments to the permanent way, full authority was given for their use with maximum loading of five coaches. This permitted the worst of the 4-4-2Ts No. 30584 to be withdrawn in January 1961, with a final mileage of 2,102,781, the other two working turn and turn about with the LMR 2-6-2Ts.

By the end of March 1961 only one of the trio of Adams 4-4-2Ts remained at Exmouth Junction and the branch workings had been taken over by Ivatt '2MT' 2-6-2Ts. No. 30584 was dead at Eastleigh stripped of collector's items such as works plates and whistle and was soon joined by No. 30583. No. 30582 made a journey to Exmouth with the Westward Television exhibition train on 11th March and then travelled to London to haul the Railway Enthusiasts' Club Waterloo to Windsor and Guildford railtour train on 19th March before returning to Exmouth Junction on 22nd March 1961.

Nos. 30582 and 30583 were then laid aside for scrapping by July 1961 and No. 30582 had been cut up at Eastleigh in March 1962 with a total mileage of 2,070,918. No. 30583 with a total mileage of 1,504,703 was purchased by the Bluebell Railway on 9th July 1961, where it is restored to working order as LSWR No. 488. Bournemouth Railway Club considered preserving one as a static exhibit but wiser counsels prevailed.

LSWR No.	1st SR No.	2nd SR No.	BR No.	*Withdrawn*
125	E0125	3125	30582	July 1961
419	–	–	–	November 1921
486	E0486	–	–	January 1928
488	–	3488	30583	July 1961
520	E0520	3520	30584	January 1961
521	–	–	–	April 1925

A fine view of '415' class 4-4-2T No. 30583 with early 'lion and wheel' emblem on the side tanks on 17th August, 1954. R.M. Casserley

A close-up of '415' class No. 30584 standing by the buffer stops at Lyme Regis in 1959 prior to running round her train. The locomotive carries the Exmouth Junction shed plate '72A' on the smokebox door and a wooden shield by the cab opening to provide enginemen with some protection from the elements on the exposed line. J. Tarrant/Kidderminster Railway Museum

LOCOMOTIVES AND ROLLING STOCK 127

The initial principal dimensions of the '415' class were:

Cylinders		17½ in. x 24 in.
Motion		Stephenson with slide valves
Heating surface		
Tubes	201 x 1¾ in.	949.0 sq. ft
Firebox		104.0 sq. ft
Total		1,053.0 sq. ft
Bogie wheels		3 ft 0 in.
Coupled wheels		5 ft 7 in.
Radial wheels		3 ft 0 in.
Wheelbase		29 ft 5 in.
Coupled wheelbase		8 ft 6 in.
Boiler		
Diameter		4 ft 2 in.
Length		10 ft 0 in.
Firebox		6 ft 2 in.
Grate area		18.25 sq. ft
Boiler pressure		160 psi
Water capacity		1,000 gallons
Coal capacity		2 tons
Weight in working order		54 tons 17 cwt
Max. axle loading		16 tons 8 cwt
Tractive effort		14,920 lb.

Later builds of Robert Stephenson had the following minor differences:

Heating surface	
Tubes	945.0 sq. ft
Firebox	111.0 sq. ft
Total	1,056.0 sq. ft
Grate area	18.0 sq. ft
Water capacity	1,250 gallons
Max. axle loading	17 tons 3 cwt
Weight in working order	58 tons 7 cwt

The locomotives fitted with Drummond boilers had yet further differences:

Boiler diameter	4 ft 2 in.
Boiler length	10 ft 1 in.
Firebox	6 ft 2 in.
Heating surface	
Tubes	1,006.0 sq. ft
Firebox	103.0 sq. ft
Total	1,109.0 sq. ft
Grate area	17.6 sq. ft
Weight in working order	58 tons 9 cwt

Another variation was that Nos. 30582 and 30584 were fitted with double slide bars whilst No. 30583 retained single slide bars. An unofficial modification during the winter months was made by footplate crews positioning wooden shields at the cab side to protect themselves from inclement weather.

Ex-GWR '14XX' class No. 1462 entering Lyme Regis with a test trip working from Axminster on 12th November, 1958. The locomotive lost so much time when working the empty stock that the trials were considered a failure. *S.C. Nash*

Ex-GWR class '14XX' 0-4-2T No. 1462 departs Lyme Regis with her three-coach test train at 12 noon on 12th November, 1958. The three coach set No. 960 proved too much for the locomotive, which failed miserably during the trials. Later members of the class worked the neighbouring Seaton branch with success in the dying years of steam traction. *S.C. Nash*

LOCOMOTIVES AND ROLLING STOCK 129

In the final years and after many minor modifications the final weights were:

Locomotive	30582	30583	30584
Max. axle loading	19 tons 1 cwt	18 tons 12 cwt	18 tons 8cwt
Weight in working order	55 tons 9 cwt	55 tons 5 cwt	56 tons 3 cwt

As the maximum permitted weight allowed on the Lyme Regis branch was 55½ tons No. 30584 had been exceeding the limit for some 35 years.

Meanwhile a possible replacement locomotive was again sought and in 1958 a candidate arrived in the form of ex-Great Western Railway '14XX' class 0-4-2 tank engine No. 1462 which began trials over the line on 11th November in charge of locomotive inspector Sam Smith of Exmouth Junction. On the first day trips were confined to light engine running for clearance tests but the following day special empty stock trains were hauled, departing Axminster at 9.06 and 11.00 am and returning from Lyme Regis at 9.33 am and 12.00 noon. With two coaches No. 1462 lost so much time with the 9.06 am departure that it was unable to return at 9.33 am and No. 30584, the branch engine, had to take the one-coach branch train to Axminster leaving No. 1462 to form the 10.00 am passenger train from Lyme Regis. Little success was achieved with No. 1462 on the second trip hauling three coaches when she lost time throughout the journey. With these poor results No. 1462 retired having achieved as little success as the previous 0-4-2 tank locomotives, the 'D1' class, almost 20 years earlier.

GWR No.	GWR 1946 No.	BR No.	Withdrawn
4862	1462	1462	September 1962

As mentioned above after suitable trials the Ivatt LMS-designed 2-6-2 tank locomotives were drafted to work the branch services and the following were known to have worked across the branch:

LMS No.	BR No.	Built	Withdrawn
1206	41206	December 1946	March 1966
	41216	September 1948	March 1966
	41223	October 1948	March 1966
	41238	September 1949	April 1965
	41270	September 1950	April 1965
	41272	September 1950	October 1965
	41284	November 1950	March 1967
	41291	September 1951	February 1966
	41292	September 1951	September 1963
	41295	October 1951	April 1967
	41297	October 1951	October 1963
	41299	November 1951	October 1966
	41306	April 1952	December 1963
	41307	April 1952	March 1966
	41308	April 1952	February 1965
	41309	May 1952	December 1963
	41318	June 1952	October 1963
	41320	January 1952	July 1967
	41321	February 1952	July 1965
	41322	February 1952	June 1964
	41323	March 1952	June 1964

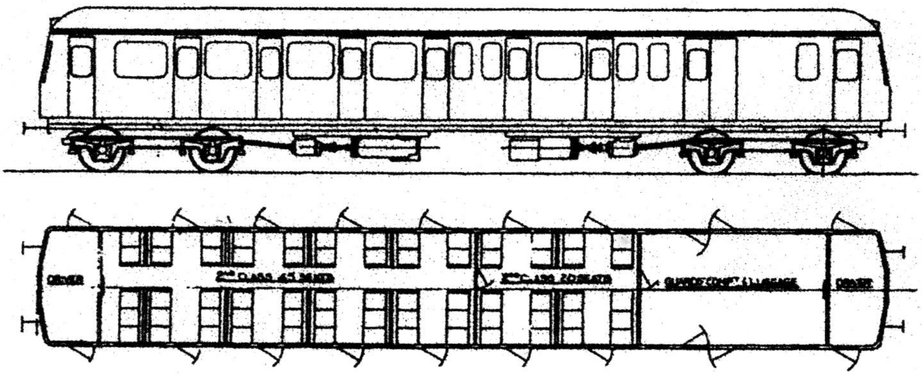

Class '122' driving motor brake second single car
built by
Gloucester Railway Carriage & Wagon Co.

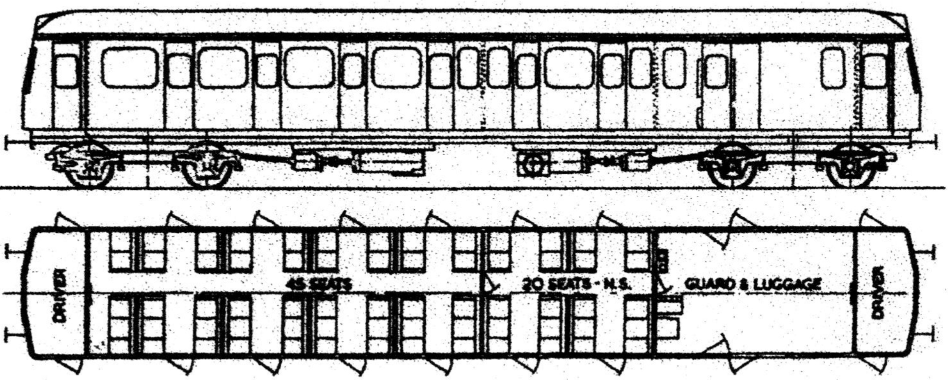

Class '121' driving motor brake second single car
built by
Pressed Steel

The leading dimensions of the LMR 2-6-2 tank locomotives were:

Cylinders		16 in. x 24 in.
		16½ in. x 24 in.*
Motion		Walschaerts valve gear
Heating surface		
Tubes	162 x 1⅝ in.	924.5 sq. ft
Firebox		101.0 sq. ft
Sub-total		1,025.5 sq. ft
Superheater	12 x 5⅛ in.	134.0 sq. ft
Total		1,159.5 sq. ft
Bogie wheels		3 ft 0 in.
Coupled wheels		5 ft 0 in.
Trailing wheels		3 ft 0 in.
Wheelbase		30 ft 3 in.
Coupled wheelbase		13 ft 9 in.
Length over buffers		38 ft 9½ in.
Boiler		
Diameter		4 ft 3 in. increasing to 4 ft 8 in.
Length		10 ft 9⅞ in.
Grate area		17.5 sq. ft
Boiler pressure		200 psi
Water capacity		1,350 gallons
Coal capacity		3 tons
Weight in working order		63 tons 5 cwt
Tractive effort		17,410 lb.
		18,510 lb.*

* For locomotives 41290 to 41329

Thereafter the LMR 2-6-2Ts handled all the services but from 4th November, 1963 they in turn were displaced by two-car diesel-multiple-units on passenger services. A shortage of diesel units however brought the return of a 2-6-2T when No. 41295 worked the branch traffic in October 1964, and for a short period from 15th February, 1965 former GWR '14XX' class 0-4-2 tank locomotives and push/pull sets were sent to cover the Seaton and Lyme Regis branches. For the duration Nos. 1442 and 1450 were transferred from Yeovil Junction shed to Exmouth Junction and although they worked the Seaton line the civil engineer prohibited their use between Axminster and Lyme Regis and 2-6-2Ts including Nos. 41216, 41223 and 41291 worked the service with push/pull units instead.

Their stay was short for when the Halwill to Torrington light railway closed in March 1965 the single car motor brake second diesel units, which had been used in that area, were transferred to the South Devon and Dorset branches including Lyme Regis. Those built by the Gloucester Railway Carriage & Wagon Co. and numbered W55000/1/11/14-17 were powered by two 150 hp 6-cylinder engines and weighed 36 tons, whilst Pressed Steel Co. built units numbered W55025/6/31 with similar engines weighed 37 tons 8 cwt. Both types seated 65 passengers and when not working singly were supplemented by a driving trailer car (unpowered). These units continued to work the branch for the remaining months until closure, augmented by 3-car dmus.

The leading dimensions of these single units were:

Lyme Regis engine shed

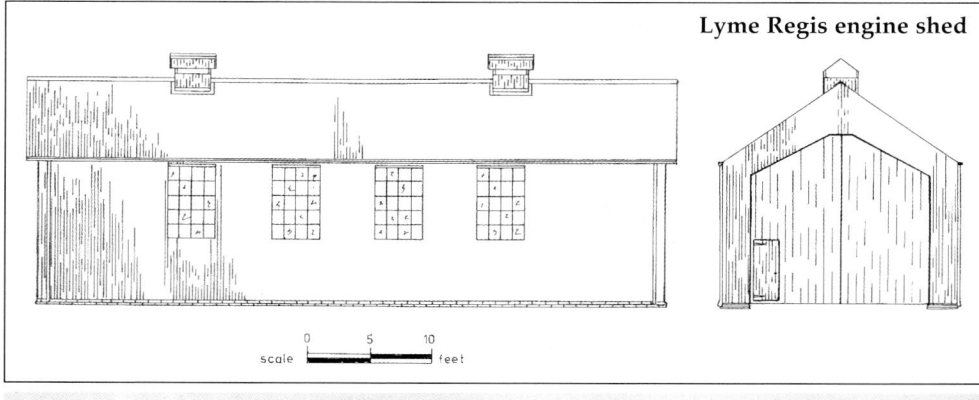

Above: The forlorn and weathered engine shed at Lyme Regis in March 1961 with the coaling stage to the right.
Author's Collection

Right: Lyme Regis engine shed in its dilapidated state in the final years, when due to subsidence the doors could not be closed. The inspection pit can be seen between the rails and to the right a well loaded coal stage.
A.E. West

	Gloucester RC&W	Pressed Steel
Class	122	121
Type	DMBS	DMBS
Engine	Two BUT (AEC) 6 cyl horizontal type of 150 bhp	Two BUT (AEC) 6 cyl horizontal type of 150 bhp
Transmission	Mechanical standard	Mechanical standard
Weight	36 tons	37 tons 8 cwt
Width	9 ft 3 in.	9 ft 3 in.
Body length	64 ft 6 in.	64 ft 6 in.
Max. speed	70 mph	70 mph
Coupling code	Blue square	Blue square
Seating (2nd class)	65	65

The maximum tail load of a passenger or mixed train worked by one engine on the branch was not to exceed 40 wheels or 120 tons in weight. When an assisting engine was provided the load of passenger trains could be increased to 72 wheels with the weight not exceeding 220 tons. The load of down goods trains could be made up to 48 wheels, including not more than 6 wagons of minerals. The load of up goods trains could be made up to 60 wheels, when it consisted principally of empty wagons. Passenger coaching stock was prohibited from being gravitated into the platform line or sidings at Lyme Regis station, all movements being made with an engine attached. From 1963 the LMR '2MT' tank locomotives were permitted to haul 11 wagons on down freight services and 14 wagons on the up road. In exceptional circumstances three additional vehicles were allowed in the down direction and one vehicle in the up direction if rail conditions were dry and the conveyance of the extra vehicles obviated a separate trip working.

Facilities and staff

The locomotive employed on the Lyme Regis branch was supplied by Exmouth Junction (Exeter) shed where all routine maintenance and boiler washouts were carried out. Because of the steep gradients and sharp curvature of the line it was usual for the locomotive to work boiler first from Axminster to Lyme Regis and, in the absence of a turntable, bunker first on the up road. At Lyme Regis the locomotive was housed in the engine shed which was just large enough to accommodate one Adams '415' class 4-4-2T. This was built of asbestos-clad corrugated-iron sheeting over a steel frame at a cost of £400 after the original timber structure, which was twice the length (100 ft by 20 ft) to accommodate two locomotives, was destroyed by fire during the night of 27th/28th December, 1912. The shed contained an inspection pit. Alongside the shed were the coaling stage and water column. By the end of World War II the building was described as 'decrepit' - some of the asbestos cladding having parted company from the structure - so in 1947 as part of general improvements at Lyme Regis the missing portions of cladding were replaced and the doors and windows painted.

Water was also available from a crane fed from the water storage tank beside the bay platform at Axminster, where a small coal stage was also installed in 1918. The water tank was constantly giving trouble and enlargement was mooted but the provision of a Vulcan hydraulic pump in the winter of 1921/22 and the improved supply rendered enlargement unnecessary. The engine crews preferred taking water at Axminster as the supply was of a better quality than at Lyme Regis.

The strangest vehicle to be found at Lyme Regis was departmental coach No. DM 198930, which was stabled in the goods yard for several years to serve as a dormitory coach for engine crews on lodging turns. The 41 ton, 65 ft 6 in. coach dated from 1904 and was one of a batch of 15 LNWR 12-wheel sleeping cars for the West Coast Joint Stock. It was original numbered 325 but at Grouping became LMS No. 10351 and then No. 470. It was withdrawn from operational stock in 1941 and transferred to departmental status. Similar coaches were employed at Wadebridge, Launceston, Bude and Seaton. Painted light grey it was withdrawn in February 1958. *L. Elsey*

After spending one week on the line, usually Saturday to Saturday, the relieved engine returned to Exmouth Junction shed to be replaced by the fresh engine ferried each way by Exmouth Junction men. On summer Saturdays when two locomotives were required for the through trains to and from Waterloo, Exmouth Junction men also worked the relief engine and relieved engine from and to Exmouth Junction and on the branch. The headcode carried by the locomotive was universal to LSWR, SR and BR route code of one white disc by day and one white light at night and during fog and falling snow above the centre of the buffer beam. Exmouth Junction duty 583, then 492, later 502, covered the Lyme Regis branch and it was usual for the locomotive to display the duty number on the white head disc.

Two sets of footplate staff were stationed at Lyme Regis on early and late turns with a cleaner and later a coalman on nights for coaling and other residual duties. Lyme Regis men signed the 'route sheets' for the branch and also 'signed the road' to Exeter and Yeovil. Lyme Regis depot was closed on and from 4th November, 1963 when staff were transferred to other depots. When the railcar service operated the unit or units were worked out from Exeter each day in the morning to work on the branch returning in the evening to the cathedral city. Two drivers spent much of their career at Lyme Regis; H.A. Fewins joined the LSWR in 1899 and was on the branch from 1917 until retirement in 1950. G.F. Hawker joined the LSWR in 1890 as a cleaner at Plymouth, fireman at Guildford and Exeter, became a driver when 29 years of age and came to the Lyme Regis branch on its opening in 1903 as a passed fireman and was made driver-in-charge the following year, a post he held until retirement in 1938. He had been appointed a local Justice of the Peace in 1933. One of the initial drivers at Lyme Regis was S. Dyer who retired six months after the opening of the line. The footplate crews in the latter years of steam working were driver Tom Woodman, fireman Vic Summers or Terry Guppy, driver George William Johns and fireman Grenville Morgan. The cleaner on nights working from 10.00 pm to 6.00 am completed the disposal routine, emptying ashes from the firebox and then prepared the locomotive coaling the bunker and filling the side tanks with water, for the next day's work. On one occasion the regulator gland was blowing and as he built up the fire boiler pressure increased and the locomotive moved as the hand brake had been inadvertently left off. The cleaner with great presence of mind screwed the handbrake hard on before the engine demolished the buffer stops and the asbestos end of the shed.

Relief footplate staff were sent from Exmouth Junction shed to Lyme Regis to cover for sickness or holidays, the driver being in effect a passed fireman and the fireman a passed cleaner to enhance their number of driving or firing turns to gain promotion. The outbased reliefmen could not cycle home from Lyme Regis to Exeter at night or claim overnight expenses so for many years they were given overnight accommodation in the former London & North Western Railway 12-wheeled sleeping car No. DM 198930 stabled in the back road at Lyme Regis goods yard. When this vehicle was scrapped in 1958 the men were forced to sleep in the goods office. Here three bunks were provided with the station porter handing out a mattress and pillowcases to each man. A coal fire was provided in the corner of the room, which was sometimes used for cooking. The normal course of events found the men going to the town for a pub meal or fish and chips followed by a pint or two in the Victoria Hotel near the station or another hostelry. One passed fireman enjoyed his outbased stint and regularly volunteered to provide holiday cover as he worked during the evening behind the bar of the Victoria Hotel, supplementing his relief allowance, whilst enjoying a comfortable bed and taking advantage of a well-cooked evening meal and breakfast. The local footplate staff were devoted to duty, for in the winter of 1962/63, one driver and fireman came across the fields each day from Axbridge near Seaton taking a circuitous route to dodge the snowdrifts which littered the area. Another came from Kilmington, west of Axminster. Local footplate crews also carried out acts of kindness for the scattered community living along the lineside. A daily paper was thrown out by the crew of the 10.05 am ex-Lyme Regis to an elderly couple who lived in a cottage on the down side of the line near Cannington viaduct whilst another was thrown to a gentleman living near Hartsgrove bridge.

On the branch drivers of up and down trains were required to sound the engine whistle continuously from a point 200 yards from and until reaching Great Trill crossing between Axminster and Combpyne.

In the event of a mishap or accident Exmouth Junction breakdown vans were allowed across the branch, but for minor incidents two travelling jacks were retained at Lyme Regis engine shed. Because of weight restrictions steam breakdown cranes were totally prohibited from the line.

Lyme Regis engine shed on the down side of the line with '415' class No. 30583 running round her train. The shed dated from 1913 after the original structure was destroyed by fire. Note the coal stage located by the shed and the water column which allowed locomotives to be watered from the shed road or run-round loop.

W. Potter/Kidderminster Railway Museum

Coaching stock

The initial coaching stock used on the light railway were LSWR 4-wheel, 4-compartment composites measuring 24 ft 6 in. together with two 2- or 3-compartment brake thirds each measuring 28 ft, usually formed three or four vehicles to a train. These sufficed until after World War I when the LSWR introduced six-wheel brake thirds and six-wheel composites formed three vehicles to a train. In the period after the takeover by the LSWR the branch train often consisted of a 45 ft brake composite and 42 ft long brake third, the latter with 7 ft bogies and 27 ft 9 in. bogie centres. A six-wheel full brake was also used in the 1920s.

A decade later these vehicles were superseded by ex-LSWR 8-compartment bogie thirds, 5-compartment brake/composites and 5- or 6-compartment brake thirds and finally by 61 ft 7 in. rebuilds. During the winter months one brake/composite sufficed but in summer a bogie third and bogie brake/composite was the usual formation, except on Saturdays.

After World War II a motley collection of ageing vehicles was drafted to the line, including ex-LSWR 10-compartment thirds, eight-compartment composites and eight-compartment brake thirds. A 48 ft composite rebuilt as a 58 ft brake composite to diagram 758 was working on the branch in the 1950s.

By 1958 a two-coach set formed of Maunsell corridor brake composite to diagram 2401 and measuring 59 ft by 9 ft and 9 ft 7 in. over the guard's lookout and former SECR 10-compartment non-corridor coach was allocated to the branch numbered in the series set 100 to 110. The following year the ex-SECR vehicle was replaced by a Maunsell open second with 59 ft body which was 9 ft wide. Set 101 comprising composite brake No. 6906 to diagram 2402 and open third, later second (No. 1300 to diagram 2007) and Set 108 comprising composite brake No. 6590 to diagram 2401 and open third, later second (No. 1310 to diagram 2007) was used in the last years of operation. On the branch it was the normal practice in winter months to use the corridor brake composite, with an open second being held at Lyme Regis as spare for strengthening purposes.

In the latter days of steam traction Maunsell corridor composite stock replaced the ex-LSWR coaches, and on summer Saturdays Bulleid and BR standard Mark I corridor coaching stock were utilized on the through services to and from Waterloo.

Camping coaches were provided at Combpyne from 1947, stabled at the end of the siding. Initially a former London, Chatham & Dover Railway 6-wheel vehicle numbered 1 in the SR camping coach fleet was based at the country station but in 1954 it was replaced by a converted ex-LSWR 56 ft bogie non-corridor composite coach built at Eastleigh in 1906 and numbered S38S. It returned to Eastleigh for maintenance after the summer period and was fitted with a wagon type hand brake lever. The Western Region takeover on the Lyme Regis branch at the end of 1962 had no immediate effect but 1963 proved to be the last year of the camping coach.

On all branch trains during Southern and BR days it was customary for a destination board bearing the legend 'Lyme Regis Branch', black lettering on a white ground, later green on white, to be carried on the bracket on the coachside body.

The livery of coaching stock in LSWR days was salmon pink upper panels and brown lower panels and ends. The SR adopted Maunsell sage/olive green for coaching stock livery after Grouping but from 1937 this was replaced by malachite green. In all cases the ends of the vehicles and underframe was black. Southern green continued after nationalization but for a short period, the suburban non-gangway stock and parcels vans were painted carmine red, some with gold and black lining

LOCOMOTIVES AND ROLLING STOCK

again with underframing black. Some of the main line stock on through trains from Waterloo was painted cream and carmine but in the last years most had reverted to green livery including the new BR Mark I corridor stock.

Exmouth Junction crews sent to relieve on the branch when Lyme Regis men were on holiday or sick were expected to lodge at Lyme Regis. For some years accommodation was made available in Departmental coach DM 198930 bearing the inscription 'Motive Power Department - Lyme Regis' on its side panels, which languished by the buffer stops in back road. The vehicle was originally one of fifteen 12-wheel sleeper coaches built in 1904 for the West Coast Joint Stock and was numbered 325 but at the Grouping was taken into LMS stock and renumbered 10351. The 65 ft 6 in., 41 ton coach was later renumbered 470 before being withdrawn from traffic stock in December 1941 and transferred for departmental use. In its final years it was painted light grey and was withdrawn in February 1958. The Southern appeared to absorb several of the same type of coach for sister vehicles were used as dormitory coaches at Bude, Launceston, Seaton and Wadebridge.

Wagons

The early wagons used by the LSWR were wooden open vehicles with side doors and fitted with dumb buffers. Where grain, straw or merchandise were susceptible to wet weather, a tarpaulin sheet was used to cover the contents of the wagon. Very few of these wagons existed at the time of the opening of the light railway and so the LSWR utilized several types of open wagon for the conveyance of general merchandise and minerals. These were 4- and 5-plank, 10-ton capacity opens to SR diagram 1309 measuring 18 ft 4 in. over buffers, 15 ft 4 in. over headstocks, with 9 ft 0 in. wheelbase, 7 ft 11 in. width and 3 ft 1 in. diameter wheels. Overall height to the top of the curved ends was 7 ft 11¼ in. on the 5-plank and 8 ft 0¼ in. on the 4-plank vehicles. Later 5-plank 10-ton capacity opens with steel underframe to SR diagram 1310 were used with 18 ft 4 in. length over buffers, 15 ft 4 in. length over headstocks, 9 ft 0 in. wheelbase, width of 7 ft 11 in., 8 ft 1¾ in. height to top of curved ends and 3 ft 1 in. diameter of wheels. Another variation was the use of 10 ton 5-plank opens with timber underframe and straight ends to SR diagram 1313, measuring 19 ft 0 in. over buffers, 16 ft 0 in. over headstocks, 9 ft 0 in. wheelbase, 6 ft $10^{13}/_{16}$ inches height and overall width of 7 ft 11½ in. Larger capacity vehicles included 12- and 15-ton capacity 8-plank opens to SR diagram 1316 measuring 21 ft 0 in. over buffers, 18 ft 0 in. over headstocks, 10 ft 6 in. wheelbase, width 7 ft 11 in., height 8 feet $8^{3}/_{16}$ in. and 3 ft 1 in. diameter wheels. Another 8-plank 12-ton capacity variant with steel underframe was to SR diagram 1314 measuring 20 ft 0 in. over buffers, 17 ft 0 in. over headstocks, 9 ft 6 in. wheelbase, 8 ft 7½ in. height, 8 ft 0 in. width and 3 ft 2 in. diameter wheels.

For perishable and fruit traffic 10-ton covered wagons with timber underframe to SR diagram 1409 were provided, measuring 21 ft 0 in. over buffers 18 ft 0 in. over headstocks with 10 ft 6 in. wheelbase and overall height of 11 ft 9¼ in., width of 8 ft 0 in. and 3 ft 1 in. diameter wheels. Later 10-ton capacity covered goods vans with steel underframe to SR diagram 1410 were also utilized. They measured 21 ft 0 in. over buffers, 18 ft 0 in. over headstocks, 10 ft 6 in. wheelbase, 11 ft 0½ in. overall height, 7 ft 9½ in. width and 3 ft 1 in. diameter wheels. A third variation was the 10-ton capacity covered goods wagon with steel underframe to SR diagram 1407, which measured 21 ft 0 in over buffers, 18 ft 0 in. over headstocks, whilst maintaining 10 ft 6 in. wheelbase, overall height of 11 ft 7¾ in., 7 ft 9½ in. width and 3 ft 1 in. diameter wheels.

For the occasional cattle traffic conveyed across the branch three types of cattle wagon would have been utilized. The first of 10-ton capacity was to SR diagram 1506 and was 21 ft 8½ in. over buffers, 18 ft 8½ in. over headstocks, had a 10 ft 6 in. wheelbase and overall height of 11 ft 2 in., width 8 ft 1¾ in. and 3 ft 1 in. diameter wheels. The second to SR diagram 1507 was also of 10-ton capacity and measured 21 ft 0 in. over buffers 18 ft 0 in. over headstocks, with 10 ft 6 in. wheelbase, overall height of 11 ft 2 in., width of 7 ft 8½ in. and 3 ft 1 in. diameter wheels. The third LSWR variant of cattle wagon to SR diagram 1502 was of 8-tons capacity 22 ft 1½ in. over buffers, 18 ft 8½ in. over headstocks, 11 ft 0 in. wheelbase and overall height of 11 ft 8 in., width 8 ft 1¾ in. and 3 ft 5 in. diameter wheels.

At the tail of the train was usually a 10 ton goods brake van (road van) to SR diagram 1541 measuring 21 ft 0 in. over buffers, 18 ft 0 in. over headstocks, 10 ft 6 in. wheelbase, 11 ft 2 in. overall height excluding chimney, 7 ft 9½ in. width and 3 ft 1 in. diameter wheels. Later a regular 20-ton capacity brake van to SR diagram 1545 was allocated for branch duties including No. S54981, formerly LSWR No. 6991, labelled 'not to work between Tonbridge and West St Leonards via Battle' in standard SR brown livery in 1952, and No. S54977 formerly LSWR No. 6907 of 1907 vintage in 1958, the year of its withdrawal, in light grey livery. The standard dimension of these vans was 21 ft 0 in. over buffers, 18 ft 0 in. over headstocks, 10 ft 6 in. wheelbase, 11 ft 3¾ in. overall height excluding chimney, 8 ft 7½ in. over guard's ducket and 3 ft 1 in. diameter wheels. Another brake van used on the branch in the years prior to World War II was former LBSCR 15-ton vehicle No. 55865 to SR diagram 1574, which was popular with guards as it had a certain similarity to LSWR brake vans. The leading dimensions were 21 ft 0 in. length over buffers, 18 ft 0 in. length over headstocks, wheelbase 10 ft 6 in., width over handrails 8 ft 10 in. and maximum height 11 ft 6 in. The height to the top of the chimney was 12 ft 10¾ in.

In addition many wagons owned by other railway companies were used to deliver and collect agricultural and livestock traffic, whilst the relatively small amounts of coal and coke supplies came in private owner coal wagons. These fell into two categories, those belonging to the collieries consigning the coal and merchants and coal factors wagons, which were loaded at the collieries.

After Grouping the LSWR wagons continued to be utilized and SECR and LBSCR wagons soon infiltrated into the system. Gradually SR-designed standard wagons made an appearance. The most numerous were probably the 12-ton 8-plank opens to diagram 1379, with 9 ft 0 in. wheelbase and measuring 17 ft 6 in. over headstocks, 20 ft 6 in. over buffers and with a width of 7 ft 11 in. and height of 8 ft 7⅞ in. Another open used was 10-ton capacity 5-plank to diagram 1380, with 9 ft 0 in. wheelbase, measuring 17 ft 6 in. over headstocks, 20 ft 6 in. over buffers and with a maximum width of 7 ft 11 in. Another variant was 12-ton, 8-plank open with 9 ft 0 in. wheelbase to diagram 1385. These measured 17 ft 6 in. over headstocks, 20 ft 6 in. over buffers, had a maximum width of 7 ft 11 in. and height of 8 ft 7⅞ in. Later variations included a 12-ton capacity 8-plank open wagon to diagram 1400, with 10 ft 0 in. wheelbase, measuring 17 ft 6 in. over headstocks and 20 ft 6 in. over buffers with maximum width of 7 ft 11 in. and height of 8 ft 7¾ in. Last came the 13-ton, 5-plank open to diagram 1375, with 10 ft 0 in. wheelbase, measuring 17 ft 6 in. over headstocks, 20 ft 6 in. over buffers, with a width of 8 ft 0 in. and maximum height of 7 ft 2⅞ in. All were used for general merchandise, vegetable and root crop traffic as well as for coal and coke. Occasional use was made of the 12-ton capacity flat truck for containers to diagram 1382, with 9 ft 0 in. wheelbase and measuring 17 ft 6 in. over headstocks and 20 ft 11 in. over buffers, used on general merchandise traffic. Fitted and unfitted 12-ton, 9 ft 0 in. wheelbase covered vans with equal planking to diagram 1428 conveyed perishable goods and fruit. These measured 17 ft 6 in. over headstocks and had a wheelbase of 20 ft 11 in. A second 12-ton capacity variant with unequal planking to diagram 1455, with 10 ft 0 in. wheelbase was also used. These were 17 ft 6 in. over headstocks, 20 ft 6 in. over buffers and had a maximum height of 12 ft 2$^{13}/_{16}$ inches. The ever decreasing amount of cattle traffic would have arrived and departed in the early style of cattle wagon to diagram 1529 with 10 ft 6 in. wheelbase and measuring 19 ft 0 in. over headstocks, 22 ft 5 in. over buffers, with maximum width of 8 ft 4¾ inches and height of 11 ft 3¾ in. The later style to diagram 1530 had 10 ft 6 in. wheelbase and measured 19 ft 0 in. over headstocks but was 22 ft 1 in. over buffers, was 8 ft 4¾ in. in width and had a height of 11 ft 3¾ in. SR standard goods brake vans infiltrated the branch and consisted of three types: 25-ton capacity to diagram 1578 and 1579 both with 16 ft 0 in. wheelbase and measuring 24 ft 0 in. over headstocks and 27 ft 0 in. over buffers, with a maximum width of 8 ft 6 in. over the guard's ducket and height of 11 ft 5⅛ in. The third type was of 15-tons capacity to diagram 1581 with similar dimensions but a maximum height of 11 ft 1⅞ in. After nationalization many of the older wooden bodied wagons were scrapped and much of the traffic conveyed in open wagons was transported in 16-ton all-steel mineral vehicles.

In LSWR days the body, solebars and headstock of open wagons and vans were painted dark brown with white lettering, whilst the ironwork below solebar level, buffer guides, buffers, drawbars, drawbar plates and couplings were black. Brake vans were also dark brown with vermilion ends and white roofs. The SR wagon livery continued the tradition of the LSWR of dark brown with white lettering with the brake vans painted the same save that the headstocks, veranda ends and inner body ends were painted Venetian red. BR livery was grey for non-fitted vehicles and bauxite for all brake-fitted stock.

The following service vehicles were prohibited from the Axminster to Lyme Regis branch:

Diagram	Vehicle
471	30 ton bogie bolster wagon
572	20 ton sleeper and ballast wagon (Grampus)
583	20 ton hopper ballast wagon (Mackerel)
642	50 ton bogie rail wagon (Salmon)
—	50 ton bogie rail sleeper and ballast utility wagon (Sturgeon)
SR 1598	40 ton Borail wagon (Permitted provided load does not exceed 20 tons uniformly distributed)
SR 1735	40 ton hopper wagon

In the event of a defect to carriages or wagons on the branch the carriage and wagon examiner based at Axminster attended and rectified the fault. More serious problems required the vehicle to be returned to Exeter. The examiner also covered the Chard and Seaton branches and intermediate sections of the main line. From 1952 the area was extended from Chard Junction to Thornfalcon.

As breakdown cranes were prohibited from the branch in the event of an emergency Exmouth Junction could use tool vans, latterly Nos. DS1555, DS1558 and DS1774, to cater for any emergencies. All were equipped with oxy-acetylene apparatus.

Appendix One

Bridges

No.	Location	Mileage (m. ch.)	Local name	Under or over	Type	Spans No.	Dimensions of span on square ft. in.	Dimensions of span on skew of girder or arch ft. in.	Max. height from ground or rail level to underside or arch ft. in.	Max. height from ground or rail level to soffit ft. in.	Type of construction
	Axminster station	0 00									
1	Axminster & Combpyne	00 15	Gamberlake	Under	Footpath	1	5 0			7 6	Concrete covered brick arch and abutments
1A	Axminster & Combpyne	00 16	Culvert	Under	Stream	1	5 3			3 0	Concrete covered brick arch and abutments
2	Axminster & Combpyne	00 25	Flyover	Under	Railway	1	25 4	35 6	14 3		Plate girder and wrought iron trough decking, concrete abutments (also No. 444C on main line)
3	Axminster & Combpyne	00 45	Shool's	Under	Private	1	12 0	13 0		9 0	Wrought iron trough decking and concrete covered brick abutments
3A	Axminster & Combpyne	00 51½	Culvert	Under	Stream	1	3 6 dia.				Concrete barrel
4	Axminster & Combpyne	00 62	Abbey Lane	Under	Public	1	12 0	13 0		16 0	Concrete covered brick arch and abutments
5	Axminster & Combpyne	00 64	Musbury Road	Under	Public	1	20 0	24 0	14 8		Plate girders, trough decking, brick abutments
5A	Axminster & Combpyne	00 76	Culvert	Under	Stream	1	3 6 dia.				Concrete barrel
6	Axminster & Combpyne	01 53½	Great Trill	Under	Private	1	12 0	12 0		13 6	Concrete covered brick arch and abutments
6A	Axminster & Combpyne	01 64	Culvert	Under	Stream	1	4 6 dia.				Concrete covered brick barrel
7	Axminster & Combpyne	01 67½	Great Trill Farm	Under	Private	1	12 0			12 9	Concrete arch, masonry abutments
8	Axminster & Combpyne	01 79	Collier's	Over	Private	1	15 9			14 0	Concrete covered brick arch, masonry abutments
9	Axminster & Combpyne	02 25	Newland	Under	Private	1	6 0			7 6	Concrete covered brick arch, masonry abutments

No.	Parish	m	ch	Name	Over/Under	Public/Private	Spans	Span ft in	Dim 2 ft in	Height ft in	Construction
9A	Axminster & Combpyne	02	35	Culvert	Under	Private	1	6 0		7 6	Concrete barrel
10	Axminster & Combpyne	02	35½	Park Farm	Under	Private	1	12 0	12 3	12 8	Concrete covered brick arch, masonry abutments
10A	Axminster & Combpyne	02	56	Culvert	Under	Private	1	6 0		7 6	Brick barrel
10B	Axminster & Combpyne	02	71	Culvert	Under	Private	1	6 0		7 3	Brick barrel
11	Axminster & Combpyne	02	73½	Hartsgrove Cattle Creep	Under	Private	1	6 0		7 3	Concrete covered brick arch, masonry abutments
12	Axminster & Combpyne	03	07	Hartsgrove (a.k.a. Pudleylake Road)	Over	Private	1	14 8		17 0	Concrete covered brick arch, masonry abutments
13	Axminster & Combpyne	04	15	Combpyne Farm	Under	Private	1	12 0		16 2	Concrete covered brick arch, masonry abutments
	Combpyne station	04	71								
14	Combpyne & Lyme Regis	04	31	New Road (a.k.a. Trinity Hill Road)	Over	Public	1	48 0		24 6	Concrete covered brick arch, masonry abutments
15	Combpyne & Lyme Regis	04	59	Shapwick Grange Farm	Under	Private	1	12 0		18 3	Concrete covered brick arch, masonry abutments
16	Combpyne & Lyme Regis	04	74	Shapwick Cattle Creep	Under	Private	1	6 0		6 6	Brick arch, masonry abutments
17	Combpyne & Lyme Regis	05	26	Cannington Viaduct	Under	Railway	10	50 0 each		79 3	Concrete arches, piers and abutments, extends from 5m 21½ch to 5m 30½ch, length 203 yards over stream and Holcombe Road
17A	Combpyne & Lyme Regis	05	66	Culvert	Under	Private	1	6 0		7 0	Brick arch
18	Combpyne & Lyme Regis	05	73	Hook's Farm (a.k.a. Gore Lane)	Over	Public	1	14 3	16 8	13 9	Concrete covered brick arch, masonry abutments
19	Combpyne & Lyme Regis	06	11	Park's Farm Cattle Creep	Under	Private	1	6 0		6 10	Concrete covered brick arch, masonry abutments
20	Combpyne & Lyme Regis	06	14	Whalley Lane. (a.k.a. Walley Lane or Uplyme Road)	Under	Public	3	11 6 / 14 3 / 11 6	13 5 / 17 6 / 13 0	14 6	Trough decking, steel trestles, concrete abutments
21	Combpyne & Lyme Regis	06	25	Harris Cattle Creep	Under	Private	1	6 0		6 10	Brick arch, masonry abutments
22	Combpyne & Lyme Regis	06	37	Lyme Road	Over	Public	1	14 0	27 9	13 7	Trough decking, masonry abutments
	Lyme Regis station	06	59								

Appendix Two

Level Crossings

No.	Location	Mileage m. ch.		Local name	Status
	Axminster station	0	00		
1	Axminster & Combpyne	0	30	Shool's	Footpath
2	Axminster & Combpyne	1	41	Great Trill Farm	Occupation
3	Axminster & Combpyne	2	58	Park Farm	Occupation
4	Axminster & Combpyne	3	46	Musbury	Occupation
	Combpyne station	4	21		
5	Combpyne & Lyme Regis	4	46	Shapwick	Footpath
6	Combpyne & Lyme Regis	5	56	Cannington No. 1	Footpath
7	Combpyne & Lyme Regis	5	60	Cannington No. 2	Footpath
	Lyme Regis station	6	59		

With blower on, '415' class No. 30583 darkens the atmosphere on 14th July, 1955 as she approaches Lyme Regis with the 4.43pm train from Axminster, which includes a through coach from Waterloo. *LCGB/Ken Nunn*

Acknowledgements

The publication of this history would not have been possible without the assistance of many people. In particular I should like to thank,

The late R.C. (Dick) Riley
Doug Stephenson
The late George Pryer
Brian Jackson
Chris Cock for signalling items
Michael Back for signalling items
Garth Ponsonby

Also staff of the former Exmouth Junction motive power depot, Axminster and Lyme Regis station staff.

Thanks are due to the National Archives, British Railways, Southern Region, British Railways, Western Region, the House of Lords Record Office, the British Museum Newspaper Library, Devon County Record Office, Dorset County Record Office and members of the South Western Circle.

Bibliography

General Works
Bradley, D.L., *Locomotives of the London and South Western Railway*, Wild Swan
Cozens, Lewis, *The Axminster & Lyme Regis Light Railway*
Faulkner, J.N. and Williams R.A., *The LSWR in the Twentieth Century*, David & Charles
Lucking, J.H. *Railways of Dorset*, RCTS
St John Thomas, D., *Regional History of the Railways of Great Britain Vol. 1*, David & Charles
Williams, R.A., *The London & South Western Railway*, David & Charles

Periodicals
Bradshaw's Railway Guide
Bradshaw's Railway Manual
British Railways Southern Region Magazine
Buses Illustrated
Herapath's Journal
Locomotive, Carriage and Wagon Review
Railway Magazine
Railway & Travel Monthly
Railway Observer
Railway World
Railway Year Book
South Western Circular
South Western Gazette
Southern Railway Magazine
Trains Illustrated

Newspapers
Bridport News
Dorset County Chronicle

Other Sources
The Minute Books of the Axminster and Lyme Regis Railway
The Minute Books of the London and South Western Railway
The Minute Books of the Southern Railway
Working Timetables   LSWR, SR, BR (SR) and BR (WR)
Appendices to Working Timetables   LSWR, SR and BR (SR)
Miscellaneous Working Instructions   LSWR, SR and BR(SR)

Index

Abortive railway schemes, 7, 8, 11
Accidents, 41, 43, 134-5
Acts of Parliament, 5, 8, 9, 29, 31, 35
Adams '415' class, 5, 6, 41, 43, 45, 51, 57 85, 116 et seq., 133
Axe & Lyme Valleys Light Railway, 57
Axminster, 5, 6, 7, 8, 11, 13, 16, 17, 20, 23, 26, 27, 29, 33, 35, 39, 41, 45, 51, 57, 59, 65, 85, 89, 97 et seq., 133, 139, 140, 142
  Closure of signal box, 57, 89
Axminster & Lyme Regis Light Railway, 5, 6, 11, 15, 21, 26, 27, 29, 71
Baldrey & Yerburgh, Messrs, 13, 17
Beeching report, 6, 55
Blanchard, H., 41, 95
Board of Trade (later Ministry of Transport), 11, 16, 17 et seq., 27, 39, 43
Bridport, 8, 9, 29, 34
British Railways, 5,6,43 et seq., 115, 121, 136, 139
Bus competition, 33, 34, 41, 45
Bus replacement services, *see Southern National*
Camping coach, 41, 45, 51, 67, 136
Cannington viaduct, 5, 15 et seq., 51, 57, 71-3, 84, 85, 135, 141
Charmouth, 11, 29, 33, 34, 39, 73
Closure of branch, 6, 55, 57
Coal crisis (1951), 45,103
Cobb, The, 7, 8, 15, 26, 35, 51
Combpyne, 6, 8, 15, 20, 23, 26, 27, 29, 34, 39, 41, 45, 51, 55, 57, 67, 85, 89, 95, 97 et seq., 125, 136, 141, 142
  Closure of signal box, 39, 67, 71, 89
  Station master withdrawn, 95
Construction costs, 13, 15, 25
Cutting first sod, 9
Electric Tablet introduced, 27, 85
Electric Tablet withdrawn, 55, 89
Engine changeover arrangements, 107, 117, 134
Film connection, 43-5
Goods working withdrawn, 89, 112
Greenslade, R., 23, 95
Guards, withdrawal of, 6, 39

Horse bus services (railway connections), 8, 17, 26, 29
Introduction of dmus, 109, 131, 134
Investigation into viability (1952), 45
Ley, C.H., 23,31 ,95
Light Railways Act (1896), 5, 9, 11, 25
London & South Western Rly, 5, 6, 7 et seq., 29 et seq., 59, 71, 85, 89, 97, 98, 113 et seq., 136 et seq.
Lyme Regis, 5, 6, 7 et seq., 29 et seq., 39, 41, 45, 51, 55, 57, 73, 84, 85, 89, 95, 97 et seq., 115 et seq., 125, 133 et seq., 141, 142
  Engine shed closed, 134
  Engine shed destroyed, 29-30, 133
  Signal box closed, 89
  Station bus service, 35
Lyme Regis Railway Co., 8, 9
'Lyme Volcano' (landslip), 29-30, 98
Naming of *Lyme Regis* locomotive, 41, 95
Opening of line, 5, 21 et seq.
Pain, Arthur, C., 5, 13 et seq., 25, 59
Southern National (bus replacement services), 6, 35, 45, 103
Southern Railway, 5, 35 et seq., 59, 85, 89, 98, 101, 117, 121, 136 et seq.
Southern Region, *see British Railways*
Special trains, 16, 45, 51, 55, 121
Speed restrictions (branch), 5, 21, 84
Strikes, 33, 35
'Terrier' locomotives, 17, 21, 26, 45, 85, 113 et seq., 121
Through coaches, 5 et seq., 65, 98, 99, 103 107,137
TUCC, 6, 55
Western Region, *see British Railways*
World War I, 31, 33, 98, 136
World War II, 39, 41, 65, 67, 73, 97, 101, 110, 121, 133, 136,138